These truths alone

THE FIVE SOLAS OF THE REFORMATION

by Jason Helopoulos

These truths alone
The Good Book Guide to the Five Solas of the Reformation
© Jason Helopoulos, 2017. Reprinted 2017 (three times), 2023.
Series Consultants: Tim Chester, Tim Thornborough,
Anne Woodcock, Carl Laferton

Published by:
The Good Book Company

thegoodbook.com | thegoodbook.co.uk
thegoodbook.com.au | thegoodbook.co.nz | thegoodbook.co.in

ISBN: 9781784981501 | JOB-007345 | Printed in India

CONTENTS

Introduction: Good Book Guides

Every Bible-study group is different—yours may take place in a church building, in a home or in a cafe, on a train, over a leisurely mid-morning coffee or squashed into a 30-minute lunch break. Your group may include new Christians, mature Christians, non-Christians, moms and tots, students, businessmen or teens. That's why we've designed these *Good Book Guides* to be flexible for use in many different situations.

Our aim in each session is to uncover the meaning of a passage, and see how it fits into the "big picture" of the Bible. But that can never be the end. We also need to appropriately apply what we have discovered to our lives. Let's take a look at what is included:

⊕ **Talkabout:** Most groups need to "break the ice" at the beginning of a session, and here's the question that will do that. It's designed to get people talking around a subject that will be covered in the course of the Bible study.

⊕ **Investigate:** The Bible text for each session is broken up into manageable chunks, with questions that aim to help you understand what the passage is about. The **Leader's Guide** contains **guidance for questions**, and sometimes ⊗ additional "follow-up" questions.

⊙ **Explore more (optional):** These questions will help you connect what you have learned to other parts of the Bible, so you can begin to fit it all together like a jig-saw; or occasionally look at a part of the passage that's not dealt with in detail in the main study.

⊕ **Apply:** As you go through a Bible study, you'll keep coming across **apply** sections. These are questions to get the group discussing what the Bible teaching means in practice for you and your church. ⊡ **Getting personal** is an opportunity for you to think, plan and pray about the changes that you personally may need to make as a result of what you have learned.

⊕ **Pray:** We want to encourage prayer that is rooted in God's word—in line with his concerns, purposes and promises. So each session ends with an opportunity to review the truths and challenges highlighted by the Bible study, and turn them into prayers of request and thanksgiving.

The **Leader's Guide** and introduction provide historical background information, explanations of the Bible texts for each session, ideas for **optional extra** activities, and guidance on how best to help people uncover the truths of God's word.

Why study the Five Solas?

"Guard the good deposit entrusted to you," Paul said to Timothy (2 Timothy 1 v 14). Some things are of such worth that we must keep them, whatever the cost. The Reformers of the 16th century rightly valued the gospel as such a gift, and many willingly gave their lives for the cause of preserving this truth and passing it along to others.

As the Reformers looked at the European church, they saw an institution that had wandered from the heart of the gospel. And when the heart of the gospel is lost, the Christian faith is lost. Therefore, these men and women were moved to put their livelihoods, homes, fortunes, and lives on the line to restore to the church the essential teachings of the gospel. These have come down to us by five Latin phrases: *Sola Scriptura, Solus Christus, Sola Gratia, Sola Fide,* and *Soli Deo Gloria.* Translated into English, they assert that salvation is according to Scripture alone, in Christ alone, by grace alone, through faith alone, for the glory of God alone.

Each of these *Solas* proves to be essential to the gospel. We neglect them to our harm. When the church loses its understanding of these rallying cries of the Reformation, it loses the gospel. Therefore, it is imperative that we guard the good deposit that has been entrusted to us. We want our world, country, town, neighbors, homes, and our very selves to be affected and gripped by the good news of the gospel. But if we do not know and adhere to these essentials, then we have no good news to pass on. This Good Book Guide gives us the opportunity to study them together, with the prayerful aim that we might cherish this wonderful salvation and preserve its truths for the next generation.

Oh, the glories of the gospel! We have been given a good deposit. It has been entrusted to us. Let us know and delight in it.

Deuteronomy 31 – 32; 2 Timothy 3 v 14-17

SOLA SCRIPTURA:
BY SCRIPTURE ALONE

"Your word of life has been, and still remains among us, faithfully collected in the sacred registers of the holy Scripture ... the image of your glory, the law of your kingdom, the ladder of heaven, the gate of paradise, the trumpet of salvation ... the treasury of piety, virtue, wisdom, consolation, and perfection."

Theodore Beza (1519-1605)

⊕ talkabout

1. What are some of the different authorities in your life?

• What are some of the benefits of living under these authorities? What are some of the implications?

⊥ investigate

▶ **Read Deuteronomy 31 v 9-13 and 32 v 45-47**

2. What is the context of these verses (31 v 1-8)?

> **DICTIONARY**
>
> **Levi (31 v 9):** one of the tribes of Israel; all priests were Levites.
> **The ark of the covenant (v 9):** a golden chest kept at the center of the tabernacle, marking the place of God's presence.
> **The year of release (v 10):** God commanded that every seven years debtors and slaves should be released.
> **The Feast of Booths (v 10):** a yearly harvest celebration; later, it would recall Israel's nomadic life, guided by God, after he led them out of Egypt.
> **Sojourner (v 12):** traveler; guest.

• What significance does this give to Moses' words here?

3. Moses instructs the priests and elders of Israel to read the Scriptures in the hearing of the people every seven years (31 v 9-11). Why?

• What does this tell us about the nature of the Scriptures and how the people of God should view them?

• What does this tell us about the role of spiritual leaders?

4. In 32 v 45-47, what does Moses emphasize about the Scriptures?

⊟ apply

5. Moses highlights that we pass on the faith through the reading and teaching of the Scriptures. What are some of the practical implications of this emphasis for us, for example, in our homes, churches, children's ministries and outreach?

optional

⊡ explore more

Sola Scriptura v Solo Scriptura

Does Moses' emphasis on the priority of reading and teaching Scripture mean that traditions, creeds and confessions are of no use for the Christian? If they are beneficial, what help do they provide, do you think?

It is important to note that the Reformers held to *Sola Scriptura* and not *Solo Scriptura*. *Solo Scriptura* advocates a radical individualism, rejecting that the church, creeds, confessions and tradition have any authority, while embracing private judgement above all else. This finds no credence in the teaching of the Reformers or the early church.

On the other hand, *Sola Scriptura* acknowledges the authority of the church, creeds, confessions and tradition, but always as subordinate to, and only as they agree with, the Scriptures themselves. The theologian R.C. Sproul is helpful in explaining the place of biblical church tradition within the *Sola Scriptura* position:

"Although tradition does not rule our interpretation, it does guide it. If upon reading a particular passage you have come up with an interpretation that has escaped the notice of every other Christian for 2,000 years, or has been championed by universally recognized heretics, chances are pretty good that you had better abandon your interpretation." (*The Agony of Deceit*, pages 34-35)

What traditions does your local church practice? What are some traditions you practice as a Christian? Are they biblical? How have they been helpful?

▶ Read Mark 7 v 1-13

What concerns Jesus in this passage and elicits such a sound rebuke from him?

What was the error that the Pharisees and scribes were committing?

⊡ getting personal

Do you believe the word of God is sufficient for your salvation and life of faith? When do doubts begin to creep in? How do you fight such doubts?

⊌ investigate

▶ Read 2 Timothy 3 v 14-17

6. What is the significance of Paul exhorting Timothy to "continue in what you have learned and have firmly believed" (v 14)?

> **DICTIONARY**
>
> **Sacred writings (v 15):** the Old Testament Scriptures.
> **Profitable (v 16):** useful.
> **Reproof (v 16):** showing error or blame.

• What had Timothy learned (v 15)?

7. What do the Scriptures teach (v 15)?

- Do the Scriptures automatically confer salvation? If not, what do they actually do?

8. How do we know the Scriptures are true in what they teach (v 16)? (See also 2 Peter 1 v 21.)

⊡ **explore more**

optional

If the Scriptures are without error, then how do we explain errant teachings of the Scriptures or different interpretations of certain passages in the history of the church?

What do the following passages indicate?
- *2 Corinthians 2 v 17; 4 v 2*
- *2 Timothy 4 v 3-4*
- *Hebrews 5 v 11-13*
- *Romans 14 v 1-4, 17*
- *1 Corinthians 13 v 9, 12*

9. How does Paul outline the sufficiency of the Scriptures in verses 16-17?

➔ **apply**

10. In what ways does *Sola Scriptura* grant freedom to the Christian? Think about the Christian's confidence, authority and peace.

11. From these two passages, what would you say to a person who says they have found a certain tradition helpful in their Christian life and they would like you to try it?

These passages show the great gift which the Scriptures are from God to his people. But it may be there are moments when we can't say we desire them more "than gold, even much fine gold"; or that they are "sweeter also than honey and drippings of the honeycomb" (Psalm 19 v 10).

12. In those times, how can we encourage our love for the Scriptures?

⊡ **getting personal**

Do you value the Scriptures as a gift from God? Consider your past week. If you added up all the minutes, how much time did you spend in the Scriptures?

How could your Bible reading be improved (quantity and quality)?

⊡ **pray**

Thank God for:
- the gift of the Scriptures.
- the clarity and sufficiency of the Scriptures for the life of faith.
- pastors and teachers who uphold the truth of God's word.

Ask God for:
- greater personal love for the Scriptures.
- protection for your pastors and elders as they preach and teach.
- churches in your area to be filled with people who demand sound and clear preaching of God's word.

2 SOLUS CHRISTUS: IN CHRIST ALONE

Isaiah 53 v 1-12; 1 John 2 v 1-2

"Through Christ alone we are given salvation, blessedness, grace, pardon, and all that makes us in any way worthy in the sight of a righteous God."

Ulrich Zwingli (1484-1531)

⊕ talkabout

1. Identify some symbols that you recognize, and the organization or entity they represent.

⊕ investigate

▶ **Read Isaiah 53 v 1-12**

Isaiah prophesies of a great Deliverer to come. This is one of four passages identified as the Servant Songs of Isaiah (see also 42 v 1-17; 49 v 1-13; 50 v 4-11), which speak of this Deliverer. This prophecy was fulfilled in the coming of Christ. The New Testament bears thorough testimony that Christ has fulfilled Isaiah 53 (e.g. Matthew 8 v 14-17; John 12 v 37-38; Luke 22 v 35-37; 1 Peter 2 v 19-25; Acts 8 v 26-35).

2. What do verses 1-3 emphasize about Christ's life?

> **DICTIONARY**
>
> **The arm of the LORD (v 1):** God's power to deliver, support or conquer.
> **Transgressions; iniquities (v 5):** sins.
> **Chastisement (v 5):** punishment.
> **Intercession (v 12):** here, speaking to God on behalf of sinners.

3. In verses 4-6, identify the singular pronouns / possessive adjectives (he, him, his) and the plural ones (our, we, us). What are the implications of how these are used?

• Why did Christ suffer these things?

4. In verse 11, what is highlighted about Christ? Why is he alone a worthy sacrifice once for all for sinners? (See also Hebrews 10 v 1-14.)

5. How does Isaiah clearly express the sufficiency of Christ's substitutionary death for our salvation (v 4, 5, 11)?

⊙ explore more

optional

❯ Read Acts 8 v 26-35

How does this passage inform our interpretation and understanding of Isaiah 53?

How did reading Isaiah 53 lead to the very salvation of the Ethiopian eunuch?

➔ apply

6. Why is it impossible for Christians to overemphasize the cross? Why would it be accurate to say there is no gospel without the cross?

- Can you think of any practices in the history of the church that have undermined the doctrine of the sufficiency of Christ's substitutionary death for sinners? How have they done this?

- Why are these practices harmful? Why would they offend God?

7. How would you use this passage to challenge someone:
- who thinks there are many ways to God?

- who believes their sin is so great that they must add good works to Christ's work?

📟 getting personal

⊡ getting personal

Do you believe Christ's death is sufficient for your salvation? Or do you tend to try and earn God's approval by your church attendance, prayer, being good, serving others, and so on?

Do you often think upon and delight in Christ's death for you? What aspect of Christ's dying sacrifice has most recently filled you with joy?

⊙ investigate

❯ Read 1 John 2 v 1-2

8. What does John say is his purpose in writing (v 1)?

DICTIONARY

My little children (v 1): how the apostle John, a leader of the church, liked to address Christians under his care.
Advocate (v 1): Jesus speaks in support and defense of his people.
Propitiation (v 2): Jesus bears God's wrath, satisfying his justice, appeasing his anger, and turning it to favor.

• **Read Romans 7 v 15; Hebrews 12 v 1-4; James 5 v 16, 19-20.** Do Christians sin?

9. What truth should comfort us when we do sin (v 1-2)?

• What allows Christ alone to occupy this role? Why can no other individual occupy this role?

⊟ apply

10. Imagine a Christian who knows their past sins were atoned for in Christ, but struggles to believe that their most recent sins as a Christian are sufficiently provided for in Christ. How would you counsel them?

- What could this person see in your life that would help them believe the truth of your words about Christ's once-for-all atonement?

11. Why has there been a tendency in the history of the church to add to the work of Christ, do you think?

- Why should we continue to emphasize and boldly proclaim the importance of the cross?

⊡ getting personal

Read Colossians 1 v 15-23. Do you delight in the person and work of Christ above all else? Meditate upon this passage—who the Son of God is, what he did for your sake, and what he shall ever be for you.

⊡ pray

Pray through **Colossians 1 v 15-23**.

- Praise Christ for who he is, what he has done, and who he shall ever be for you.
- Thank Christ for who he is, what he has done, and who he shall ever be for you.
- Ask Christ to help you delight in who he is, what he has done, and who he shall ever be for you.
- Ask Christ to reveal who he is, what he has done, and who he shall ever be to some of your unsaved friends and family members.

3 Deuteronomy 7 v 6-8; 9 v 1-6; Ephesians 2 v 1-10
SOLA GRATIA:
BY GRACE ALONE

"Sin is not canceled by lawful living, for no person is able to live up to the Law. The Law reveals guilt, fills the conscience with terror, and drives men to despair. Much less is sin taken away by man-invented endeavors. The fact is, the more a person seeks credit for himself by his own efforts, the deeper he goes into debt. Nothing can take away sin except the grace of God. In actual living, however, it is not so easy to persuade oneself that by grace alone, in opposition to every other means, we obtain the forgiveness of our sins and peace with God."

Martin Luther (1483-1546)

⊕ talkabout

1. What is the best gift you have received (e.g. birthday, wedding, anniversary, Mother's Day, etc.)?

⊕ investigate

▶ **Read Deuteronomy 7 v 6-8**

The LORD redeemed the people of Israel from the land of Egypt through his servant Moses. The Israelites witnessed the miracles of the LORD, the parting of the waters of the Red Sea, and the destruction of the Egyptian army; yet they chose to rebel against the LORD. Therefore, the LORD would not allow that generation to enter the promised land. Instead, they wandered in the wilderness until the rebellious generation passed away. In this section of Deuteronomy, Moses instructs the nation before it proceeds to the long-awaited conquest and occupation of the promised land.

> **DICTIONARY**
>
> **Holy (v 6):** set apart to belong to God.
> **Redeemed (v 8):** deliverance from bondage based on the payment of a price by a redeemer.

2. What does it mean that God chose Israel out of all the peoples on the face of the earth (7 v 6)?

• Note that they did not choose God: God chose them. Why is this important?

3. Why were they alone of "all the peoples who are on the face of the earth" counted as "his treasured possession" and shown favor (v 7-8)?

• Where had God acted in the same way previously in Bible history?

▶ **Read Deuteronomy 9 v 1-6**

4. What did Moses remind the people of? What did he warn them against? Why is this important in the context?

⮕ apply

5. What practical importance does God's free, sovereign choice to save people by an act of gracious love have upon our preaching, teaching, and evangelizing as Christians?

⊡ getting personal

Think of people in your own life who seem "beyond salvation." What hope should this passage give to you? How should it guide your prayers?

⬇ investigate

> **❯ Read Ephesians 2 v 1-10**

6. What does Paul say about our condition before salvation (v 1-3)?

- Is this only true concerning some people? Why or why not?

DICTIONARY

Trespasses (v 1): ways of breaking the law of God.
Prince of the power of the air (v 2): Satan.
Flesh (v 3): here, the realm of humanity that is in opposition to God and dominated by sinfulness.
Wrath (v 3): the deserved, holy anger of God.
Grace (v 5,7,8): the unmerited favor of God toward man.

7. What are the implications of being *"dead* in [our] trespasses and sins"?

☺ **explore more**

optional

Look at the following passages. What does each tell us about the state of fallen people?
- *John 3 v 19-20*
- *Romans 3 v 10-18*
- *Colossians 3 v 5-7*
- *John 8 v 34*
- *Romans 8 v 6-8*

8. "Of course God will save; it is his job!" What is the problem with such a statement?

9. Why is it important to understand the depth of our sin and the wretchedness of our condition apart from Christ to truly value our salvation fully?

10. Who is the active party in verses 4-7?

- What did God accomplish for us (v 5-8)?

- Why did God choose to save us (v 4)?

- How did God choose to save us (v 8)?

11. Why should the doctrine of *Sola Gratia* put a stop to all boasting (v 9)?

⊡ apply

12. What would you say to the individual who believes that "grace alone" undermines living a life of holiness to the Lord?

- What characteristics would you expect to see in the life of someone who has grasped the truth that salvation comes to us by grace alone?

⊡ getting personal

How does understanding grace as the sovereign, free, unmerited favor of God encourage your view of God and the Christian life? How will this guide the way you live?

⊕ pray

- Pray for yourself—that God would help you to enjoy and rest in his grace more fully.
- Pray for your church—that God's grace would flow in and from your community, its preaching, teaching and ministries.
- Pray for others—that God would pour out his sovereign saving grace upon your neighbors, co-workers, friends and family members (pray for them by name).

4 Psalm 32 v 1-11; Romans 3 v 21-26
SOLA FIDE:
THROUGH FAITH ALONE

"Why is it that justification is attributed to faith alone? ... Since we are justified by the mercy of God alone, and faith is clearly the recognition of that mercy by whatever promise you apprehend it, justification is attributed to faith alone ... Therefore, when justification is attributed to faith, it is attributed to the mercy of God; it is taken out of the realm of human efforts, works, and merits."

Philip Melanchthon (1497-1560)

⊕ talkabout

1. List some popular movies, television shows, and books that involve a courtroom scene or extended trials, and share your favorite. What makes this genre of entertainment stimulating for so many people?

⊕ investigate

▶ Read Psalm 32 v 1-11

Both the preface to this psalm and the apostle Paul (in Romans 4 v 6-8) attribute this psalm to David. Most likely, David wrote it following his composition of Psalm 51, and as a reflection upon his repentance after his great sins related to Bathsheba (see 2 Samuel 11). The preface to Psalm 32 calls it a *maskil* (a teaching psalm). We should not dismiss this psalm as simply the experience of one believer (David), but rather, we are to learn from it the deep lessons of a faith-filled life. In this psalm, David presents the weak, struggling sinner with a path to help, forgiveness and peace.

> **DICTIONARY**
>
> **Blessed (v 1):** happy.
> **Transgression (v 1); iniquity (v 2):** sin.
> **Your hand (v 4):** a way of speaking about God's work or activity.

2. What two aspects of salvation does David highlight in verse 1?

3. What marks the "blessed" person? What does David mean by "blessed" (v 1-2)?

- How does this view of the "blessed" or "happy" person contrast with the world's view of the "happy" person?

4. Summarize David's transgressions (see 2 Samuel 11). Why did David feel as though his bones were wasting away, do you think (Psalm 32 v 3)?

- How did David eventually find relief and peace (v 5, 10)?

- Was David still a sinner when he found this relief? How do we know?

⊡ **explore more**

optional

> ❯ **Read Psalm 51**

Compare Psalm 51 to Psalm 32. Look for similar terms (e.g. transgressions, sin) and themes (e.g. forgiveness, the weight of guilt).

What truths here do you think might surprise someone who doesn't know the message of the Bible?

⊖ apply

5. From personal experience, what are some of the benefits you as a Christian enjoy by confessing your sins to God?

⊡ getting personal

Where does your happiness come from? From things that the world says will make you happy, or from trusting the Lord to forgive and cover all your sin?

If you can identify with David in Psalm 32 v 3-4, what do you need to do? When and how will you do that?

⊙ investigate

> ❯ **Read Romans 3 v 21-26**

Many rightly consider the book of Romans to be Paul's theological "tour de force." In chapters 1 – 11, Paul focuses in detail on the doctrine of justification by faith alone. Then, in chapters 12 – 16, Paul fleshes out what the Christian life should look like in response to this great salvation.

> **DICTIONARY**
>
> **Righteousness (v 21, 26):** in v 21, right standing before God; in v 26, morally right or justifiable.
> **The Law and the Prophets (v 21):** the Old Testament.
> **Justified (v 24):** to be right with God—not guilty in his sight.
> **Redemption (v 24):** to purchase or buy back a life.
> **Propitiation (v 25):** describes Jesus' death: it was a substitutionary sacrifice that satisfies God's wrath against sin.

Romans begins with a focus on the sinfulness of man. God is rightly moved with wrath towards all ungodliness (1 v 18). All people know there is a God, but suppress this truth in their unrighteousness (1 v 18-23). Therefore, God handed mankind over to their lusts and sin-filled desires (1 v 24-32). This sinful state is not only true of Gentiles (1 v 29-32), but also of Jews (2 v 1 – 3 v 8). The reality is that all people are unrighteous and deserving of the wrath of God (3 v 9-20). This news hangs in the air like a dark banner over mankind.

But then Paul launches into a discourse on the gospel and the great salvation that God provides by grace alone in Christ alone through faith alone. Here is the hope of salvation that all people need.

6. Why does Paul say that the "righteousness of God" has been manifested (shown) *now* (3 v 21)?

- Salvation through faith in Christ was not a new idea in salvation history (v 21-22). Why is this essential to understand?

7. Why is it impossible for people to be saved through their law-keeping (v 21, 23)? Why must the righteousness we need come from outside us?

8. Why was it necessary for salvation that there should be a propitiatory sacrifice (v 25)?

- How does the death of Jesus on the cross satisfy this need (v 26)?

- Some opponents of the gospel argue that the righteous Christ taking the place of sinners and bearing their penalty makes a mockery of law and justice. Why is that not the case?

9. What role does faith play in our salvation (v 25-26)?

- How would you reply to someone who says that faith is a work (that is, it's something we do that *merits* salvation) (v 24)?

optional

⊡ explore more

▸ Read Romans 10 v 14-17

Identify and discuss each use of the word "belief" or "faith" here.

What practical implications does this text have for:
- *the church?*
- *the individual Christian?*
- *your family?*

The Reformers defined faith as knowledge, assent, and trust. Each of these elements is necessary for saving faith.

- Knowledge—the Scriptures do not teach that salvation is by faith in faith. Possessing faith isn't enough; the object of faith is all-important. There must be true knowledge of Christ for it to be saving faith. We must know what we believe to believe in it.

- Assent—one must not only know the truth, but be convinced this truth is indeed true. We need more than intellectual understanding; saving faith includes conviction.

- Trust—saving faith knows the truth (knowledge), is convinced it is indeed true (assent), and also rests in the beauty, sweetness, and love of Christ. Note that Satan and the demons have knowledge and assent, but not trust (James 2 v 19).

⊖ apply

10. How would you explain saving faith to an individual who believes that general faith in God saves, and that one doesn't necessarily need to believe in Christ?

11. Martin Luther, the Reformer, said, "If the article [doctrine] of justification is lost, all Christian doctrine is lost at the same time." Why is he correct?

12. What comforts should mark the life of an individual who knows that they are justified by grace alone in Christ alone through faith alone?

⬆ pray

Base your prayers of praise, confession and thanks on Psalm 32.

5 Psalms 19 v 1-2; 24 v 1-2; Romans 11 v 33 – 12 v 2

SOLI DEO GLORIA:
GLORY TO GOD ALONE

"Our being should be employed for [God's] glory: for how unreasonable would it be for creatures, whom he has formed and whom he sustains, to live for any other purpose than for making his glory known? ... The whole order of things would be strangely subverted, were not God, who is the beginning of all things, the end also ... God justly claims for himself absolute supremacy, and that in the condition of mankind and of the whole world nothing is to be sought beyond his own glory. It hence follows, that absurd and contrary to reason, and even insane, are all those sentiments which tend to diminish his glory."

John Calvin (1509-1564)

⊕ talkabout

1. What are some different pursuits and goals that shape people's lives?

⊥ investigate

▶ Read Psalms 19 v 1-2 and 24 v 1-2

2. What does David mean when he says, "The heavens declare the glory of God" and, "The sky above proclaims his handiwork" (v 1)?

DICTIONARY

The heavens (19 v 1): here, it refers to the sky by day.
Glory of God (v 1): God's "weightiness"; what inherently, eternally, and inwardly marks his person.
Sky above (v 1): here, it refers to the sky by night.

- How do the day and night skies declare the glory of God and proclaim his handiwork?

- What is the importance of the repetition in "day to day" and "night to night" (v 2)?

3. Why is it fitting that all creation should exist to bring glory to God (Psalm 24 v 1-2)?

- What is the implication the psalmist derives from God creating all things (Psalm 24 v 1)?

⊡ **explore more**

optional

▶ **Read Psalm 19 v 1-14**

How else does the Lord reveal himself and what is significant about this?

→ apply

4. What is the practical significance of everything being created for the glory of God? How does this impact your life?

⊡ getting personal

Take time to go for a walk this week. Look at the things around you and ask yourself repeatedly, "How does this give glory to God?". Notice objects around you and realize that everything exists for God's glory. Think deeply about how. Return home and journal some of your thoughts and end with praying a prayer of adoration to God.

⊻ investigate

▶ Read Romans 11 v 33-36

Paul erupts with a doxology (praise of God) at the end of Romans 11. Why? In chapters 1 – 11 Paul has laid out the theology of our salvation: our helpless state as sinners under the wrath of God, God's answer in providing his righteousness through the person and work of his Son, the eternal hope of our salvation, and God's work in history to bring this salvation to Jews and Gentiles. Paul's response to all this is not to boast in this knowledge, but to glory in God. Knowing such a salvation leads to the praise and adoration of the Giver of this salvation.

5. Typically, when we don't understand something completely, it makes us uneasy and anxious. Yet Paul highlights the depths of God's wisdom and knowledge, the unsearchableness of his judgments, and the inscrutability of his ways, and instead of causing him anxiety, it leads him to praise. Why is this, do you think?

6. Why is it significant in relation to our salvation that no one has served as the Lord's counselor (v 34)?

• Why is it significant in relation to our salvation that no one "has given a gift to him that he might be repaid" (v 35)?

7. How does verse 36 echo the theology we observed in Psalms 19 and 24?

• How does this inform our understanding of the purpose of salvation?

❯ Read Romans 12 v 1-2

Notice that Paul uses the word "therefore" to introduce this section of his letter.

8. What do these verses indicate about the connection between Romans 1 – 11 and the rest of Paul's letter?

⊡ explore more

Briefly skim Romans 12 – 16. What are some of the instructions Paul gives for living to the glory of God?

9. It is essential to understand that *Soli Deo Gloria* (glory to God alone) is first about God's glory rather than about us giving him glory. Why, do you think?

10. Why would Paul say that glory should be given to God "forever" (11 v 36)?

⊡ getting personal

Do you believe your salvation has as its ultimate end the glory of God? Where is the evidence of that in your thoughts, speech, desires, living, worship, prayers? Where is there no evidence? (Commit to taking some time to write these answers down; the results may be more "eye-opening" than you expect.)

⊟ apply

11. All things are for the glory of God. In what ways should this affect our lives in the following areas?

• Marriage

• Parenting

• Recreation

• Finances

• Worship

• Work

12. How do all the other *Solas* (Scripture alone, Christ alone, grace alone, and faith alone) lead to this final *Sola*?

⊡ **pray**

Read each of the following psalms aloud, pausing between each reading for a time of prayer. Use the psalm to orient your prayers and to give glory to God alone. **Read Psalm 29; Psalm 145; Psalm 148.**

6 Psalm 78; 2 Timothy 1 v 1-14

PRESERVING AND PRESSING ON

⊕ talkabout

1. What is your family's greatest possession? If it is old, how many generations passed it down through your family? Why is this heirloom important to your family?

⊕ investigate

▶ Read Psalm 78 v 1-8

Psalm 78 holds the distinction of being the second longest psalm (Psalm 119 is first). It recounts five centuries of Israelite history from the time of Moses to the time of David. However, this isn't a bare history lesson. Asaph, the psalmist, recounts this history and exhorts the Israelite people through it to remember the great works of God, so that they might follow this great God in faithfulness.

> **DICTIONARY**
>
> **Maskil (preface):** a teaching psalm.
> **Parable (v 2):** a story designed to teach truth; in this context a historical story.

2. What does Asaph want the people to pay attention to (v 1-3)?

- What is the central theme he wants them to see in this history (v 4)?

3. What responsibility and privilege does each generation have before the LORD (v 5-6)?

⊡ **explore more**

optional

In groups, read the following sections of Psalm 78 and answer the questions.
- v 9-31
- v 32-55
- v 56-72

What is reflected in these verses about the people of God?

What is reflected in these verses about God himself?

4. Why is Asaph concerned that the next generation teach these lessons (v 7-8)?

→ **apply**

5. What are the stories that our generation should be telling the generation that comes after us?

• In what ways can we help each other to do this?

⊡ **investigate**

> ❱ **Read 2 Timothy 1 v 1-14**

The apostle Paul penned this letter to his young protégé Timothy in order to encourage him to keep the faith and contend for the gospel in the face of suffering. The subject of this letter becomes even more poignant with the realization that Paul wrote this letter while imprisoned in Rome and right before his impending death.

DICTIONARY

Apostle (v 1): a witness to the risen Christ and chosen to teach his word.
Laying on of my hands (v 6):
Testimony (v 8): message.

6. Paul is reminded of Timothy's faith (v 5). What characterizes that faith?

7. Why should every Christian mother, grandmother, father, husband, neighbor, and co-worker want to share the faith with those around them?

8. Of what is Paul "not ashamed," do you think (v 12)?

• Why is Paul not ashamed (v 12)?

9. What great assurance does Paul provide at the end of verse 12?

10. How does this assurance not lessen the responsibility that Christians bear to preserve and pass on this faith to others (v 13-14)?

⊡ **explore more**

Read the following passages from Paul's pastoral letters and discuss his concerns in them:
- *1 Timothy 6 v 3-5*
- *1 Timothy 6 v 20-21*
- *2 Timothy 3 v 14-17*
- *2 Timothy 4 v 1-5*
- *Titus 2 v 1*
- *Titus 3 v 9-11*

40   These truths alone

⊇ apply

11. Why is it essential that we communicate the doctrinal truths contained in the five *Solas* of the Reformation to the generation that follows us? What is lost if we don't?

12. How did you first hear the truths of the gospel?

- How does your story, and the stories of others in your group, motivate you all to be actively aiming to pass on the gospel yourselves?

⊡ getting personal

Are you concerned about guarding the good deposit entrusted to you? How are you preserving it? How are you passing it on? Think and pray through this area of your life.

⬆ pray

- Praise God for who he is and for his mighty works.
- Give thanks to God for his saving work in your life.
- Pray for the church—that it would faithfully preserve the gospel in this generation.
- Pray for family members, friends, and neighbors who need to hear this gospel.

These truths
alone

LEADER'S GUIDE

Leader's Guide

INTRODUCTION

Leading a Bible study can be a bit like herding cats—everyone has a different idea of what the passage could be about, and a different line of enquiry that they want to pursue. But a good group leader is more than someone who just referees this kind of discussion. You will want to:

- correctly understand and handle the Bible passage. But also...

- encourage and train the people in your group to do this for themselves. Don't fall into the trap of spoon-feeding people by simply passing on the information in the Leader's Guide. Then...

- make sure that no Bible study is finished without everyone knowing how the passage is relevant for them. What changes do you all need to make in the light of the things you have been learning? And finally...

- encourage the group to turn all that has been learned and discussed into prayer.

Your Bible-study group is unique, and you are likely to know better than anyone the capabilities, backgrounds and circumstances of the people you are leading. That's why we've designed these guides with a number of optional features. If they're a quiet bunch, you might want to spend longer on *talkabout*. If your time is limited, you can choose to skip *explore more*, or get people to look at these questions at home. Can't get enough of Bible study? Well, some studies have optional extra homework projects. As leader, you can adapt and select the material to the needs of your particular group.

So what's in the Leader's Guide? The main thing that this Leader's Guide will help you to do is to understand the major teaching points in the passage you are studying, and how to apply them. As well as guidance for the questions, the Leader's Guide for each session contains the following important sections:

THE BIG IDEA

One or two key sentences will give you the main point of the session. This is what you should be aiming to have fixed in people's minds as they leave the Bible study. And it's the point you need to head back towards when the discussion goes off at a tangent.

SUMMARY

An overview of the passage, including plenty of useful historical background information.

OPTIONAL EXTRA

Usually this is an introductory activity that ties in with the main theme of the Bible study, and is designed to "break the ice" at the beginning of a session. Or it may be a "homework project" that people can tackle during the week.

So let's take a look at the various different features of a Good Book Guide:

⟨↔⟩ talkabout

Each session kicks off with a discussion question, based on the group's opinions or experiences. It's designed to get people talking and thinking in a general way about the main subject of the Bible study.

⬇ investigate

The first thing you and your group need to know is what the Bible passage is about, which is the purpose of these questions. But watch out—people may come up with answers based on their experiences or teaching they have heard in the past, without referring to the passage at all. It's amazing how often we can get through a Bible study without actually looking at the Bible! If you're stuck for an answer, the Leader's Guide contains guidance for questions. These are the answers to direct your group to. This information isn't meant to be read out to people—ideally, you want them to discover these answers from the Bible for themselves. Sometimes there are optional follow-up questions (see ☑ in guidance for questions) to help you help your group get to the answer.

⊡ explore more

These questions generally point people to other relevant parts of the Bible. They are useful for helping your group to see how the passage fits into the "big picture" of the whole Bible. These sections are OPTIONAL—only use them if you have time. Remember that it's better to finish in good time having really grasped one big thing from the passage, than to try and cram everything in.

➔ apply

We want to encourage you to spend more time working at application—too often, it is simply tacked on at the end. In the Good Book Guides, apply sections are mixed in with the investigate sections of the study. We hope that people will realize that application is not just an optional extra, but rather, the whole purpose of studying the

Bible. We do Bible study so that our lives can be changed by what we hear from God's word. If you skip the application, the Bible study hasn't achieved its purpose.

These questions draw out practical lessons that we can all learn from the Bible passage. You can review what has been learned so far, and think about practical differences that this should make in our churches and our lives. The group gets the opportunity to talk about what they personally have learned.

⊡ getting personal

These can be done at home, but it is well worth allowing a few moments of quiet reflection during the study for each person to think and pray about specific changes they need to make in their own lives. Why not have a time for reporting back at the beginning of the following session, so that everyone can be encouraged and challenged by one another to make application a priority?

⬆ pray

In Acts 4 v 25-30 the first Christians quoted Psalm 2 as they prayed in response to the persecution of the apostles by the Jewish religious leaders. Today however, it's not as common for Christians to base prayers on the truths of God's word as it once was. As a result, our prayers tend to be weak, superficial and self-centered rather than bold, visionary and God-centered.

The prayer section is based on what has been learned from the Bible passage. How different our prayer times would be if we were genuinely responding to what God has said to us through his word.

1

Deuteronomy 31 – 32; 2 Timothy 3 v 14-17

SOLA SCRIPTURA:
BY SCRIPTURE ALONE

THE BIG IDEA

The Scriptures alone are our supreme authority in all spiritual matters. They contain, and are sufficiently clear in teaching, all things necessary for salvation and the life of faith.

SUMMARY

The Reformers of the 16th century recognized that the church had wandered away from the authority of the Scriptures. It had turned to popes, papal decrees, councils, tradition, and even mysticism as a replacement for the Bible. Yet, both the Old and New Testaments assert the authority of the Scriptures in the life of God's people. The Reformation sought to restore the primacy of this God-inspired and inerrant authority in the life of God's people. The Reformers believed and proclaimed that the Scriptures alone were ultimately authoritative and sufficiently clear to communicate all that is needed for salvation and the life of faith.

We see this teaching throughout the Old and New Testaments. In Deuteronomy 31 Moses begins to address the nation of Israel before his death. He reassures the nation that God will "go over" the Jordan before them (v 3) and will destroy the nations in the land, just as he led them in victory over the enemy kings Sihon and Og in the years before (v 4). He passes the mantle of leadership to Joshua (v 7-8) and then addresses the nation in verses 9-13. Moses' instruction to the nation in these verses focuses upon their listening to and learning from the Scriptures. God's word is to play a central role—in fact, the central role—in their life of faith.

The New Testament echoes this all-important truth. In 2 Timothy 3 v 14-17, Paul instructs his young protégé, Timothy, to teach and preach this God-breathed word to the people of God. He insists that the Scriptures are authoritative and sufficient for this young pastor in his ministry to and for the people of God.

OPTIONAL EXTRA

Find some examples of the last words of well-known people (many can be found online). You could ask the group to match the words and speakers, and/or you could discuss each example: what does this say about the person who said them? In the first part of this study, we will look at some of the final words of Moses, and think about their importance for God's people. (This links with Question 2.)

GUIDANCE FOR QUESTIONS

1. What are some of the different authorities in your life? In this study we will see that the Scriptures are the authority in matters of faith and practice. Allow the group to discuss different authorities in their lives. Explore authorities in the workplace, the home, society, recreational activities, and the church.

- **What are some of the benefits of living under these authorities? What are some of the implications?** Help the group to think through the reasons why

God ordained these authorities to exist, and the benefits and implications such authorities have for our lives.

Benefits: Order, protection, provision, guidance, example, authority, peace, etc.

Implications: It is important to recognize God-ordained authority, honor it, listen to it and even submit to it.

2. What is the context of these verses (31 v 1-8)? Moses, the great leader and deliverer of God's people, is preparing to depart in death. Help the group to understand how abrupt and monumental this change would be for the Israelites.

• **What significance does this give to Moses' words here?** Who would lead them? How would they know what to trust? The words Moses speaks in this passage, which mark his final instructions for these people he has served and loved, answer these questions. The dying words of God's servants to God's people often focus upon the essential.

Note: The Feast of Booths, also known as the Feast of Tabernacles, served as an annual celebration at the end of the agricultural season. It spoke of God's provision in the present through agricultural produce and, more importantly, looked back in remembrance to God's provision for his people in the past as they journeyed from Egypt to Canaan, the promised land. During these days of wandering, the Israelite people lived in booths (Leviticus 23 v 33-43), thus the name for the feast. This feast reminded God's people of his provision and their covenant obligation to serve him.

3. Moses instructs the priests and elders of Israel to read the Scriptures in the hearing of the people every seven years (31 v 9-11). Why? So "that they may hear and learn to fear the LORD your God, and

be careful to do all the words of this law" (v 12). Notice that they were to hear it and then to live in light of it. Knowledge informs living. In addition, Moses explicitly states that the Scriptures are to be read so that the following generation also hears it and learns "to fear the LORD your God" (v 13). This law was authoritative and sufficient to instruct the covenant people of God in living a life of faith before their God.

• **What does this tell us about the nature of the Scriptures and how the people of God should view them?** Moses offers no other means by which the people can ensure they keep living in God's way than that of listening to the law, learning to fear God and following carefully all his words. The Scriptures are clear enough in their articulation of truth that the average Christian can understand all that is necessary for salvation and the life of faith. It is important to help the group understand that not all things are equally clear in Scripture (Peter makes this point about Paul's writings in 2 Peter 3 v 16—notice he calls them Scripture), but all that is necessary for salvation and the life of faith is sufficiently clear in Scripture for everyone to understand. Notice that all the nation gathered to hear the teaching of Scripture.

• **What does this tell us about the role of spiritual leaders?** The principle of *Sola Scriptura* does not dismiss or disapprove of pastors or teachers (in fact, the Reformers would have cringed at such an attitude). God gifts, calls and ordains men to such roles. However, note that Moses' final instruction to the spiritual leaders of Israel is to charge them with teaching the word of God (as we will also see in 2 Timothy 3 v 14-17). Spiritual leaders derive their authority from the word of God alone. But when they depart from God's word or go beyond it, they lose that authority.

4. In [Deuteronomy] 32 v 45-47, what does Moses emphasize about the Scriptures? That this word is the way to life. It points them to life and is sufficient for that life. Encourage the group to take v 47 to heart. The prevailing view of Scripture in our culture is of a dusty, outdated text full of burdensome laws and restrictions. The Christian's joyful testimony abut God's word should astonish those around us.

5. APPLY: Moses highlights that we pass on the faith through the reading and teaching of the Scriptures. What are some of the practical implications of this emphasis for us, for example, in our homes, churches, children's ministries and outreach? Christian homes, Sunday schools and nurseries need to be filled with reading and teaching the Scriptures. Christian parents dare not neglect reading and teaching the Scriptures to their children or they neglect their children's souls. Family worship centered on the word of God, a Sunday-school curriculum filled with the word of God, and children's ministry saturated with the word of God benefits our children. It is their "very life" (32 v 47).

EXPLORE MORE
Does Moses' emphasis on the priority of reading and teaching Scripture mean that traditions, creeds and confessions are of no use for the Christian? If they are beneficial, what help do they provide, do you think? Traditions, creeds and confessions play an important role in the Christian faith. For example, the Apostles' Creed has long been recognized by the church as a summary of the essentials of Christianity. Creeds and confessions seek

to clearly articulate what the entire Bible says on a given subject. For example, it is not possible to turn to one passage in the Bible or one book of the Bible to define the doctrine of baptism. Whereas a creed or confession can detail what the entire Bible says about baptism by drawing on all the Scriptures.

However, our traditions, creeds and confessions are only as good as they are biblical. The Bible possesses sole authority, so where our traditions, creeds and confessions are in disagreement with the Scriptures, they are to be rejected; where they agree, we can embrace them and count them as useful in the life of the Christian.

Understanding this distinction is of paramount importance. It underscores the fact that the Scriptures alone are necessary and sufficient, whereas traditions, creeds and confessions only benefit insofar as they promote the teachings of Scripture. Scripture sits in judgment over our traditions, creeds and confessions—never the other way around.

What traditions does your local church practice? What are some traditions you practice as a Christian? Are they biblical? How have they been helpful? Help the group explore traditions such as reciting the Apostles' Creed, singing the Doxology, and having a daily quiet time of Bible reading and prayer. These are all good and fine traditions, because they are in accordance with the Scriptures. Think together through traditions that would not be acceptable or helpful (e.g. praying to Mary, going on pilgrimages, touching the relics of departed Christians), because they have no biblical warrant and prove to undermine our faith in, and the authority of, the Scriptures.

Read Mark 7 v 1-13. What concerns Jesus in this passage and elicits such a sound rebuke from him? Jesus is concerned that the Pharisees and scribes were holding to the tradition of men rather than obeying the commandments of God (v 8).

What was the error that the Pharisees and scribes were committing? They were forsaking the authoritative Scriptures for their own traditions. What was to guide their faith and practice was superseded by their "own wisdom," rather than the wisdom of God.

6. What is the significance of Paul exhorting Timothy to "continue in what you have learned and have firmly believed" (v 14)? The Christian life consists not only of a moment of belief, but a life of belief. Timothy embraced the truth he learned from the Scriptures and needed to continue in that belief.

- **What had Timothy learned (v 15)?** Timothy learned the "sacred writings" (v 15). Timothy's mother (Eunice) and grandmother (Lois) raised Timothy to know the Scriptures and the faith they proclaim (see 2 Timothy 1 v 5).

7. What do the Scriptures teach (v 15)? The Scriptures teach salvation. Note that there is nothing supplemental. The Scriptures are sufficient.

- **Do the Scriptures automatically confer salvation? If not, what do they actually do?** The Scriptures do not automatically confer salvation upon a person hearing or reading them. Rather, they teach or instruct you ("make you wise") in the way of salvation. They point to salvation and take the listener by the hand to Christ. Salvation is received as you come to Christ Jesus in faith (v 15).

8. How do we know the Scriptures are true in what they teach (v 16)? (See also 2 Peter 1 v 21.) They are "breathed out by God." Help the group to understand the importance of this phrase. It speaks of the source of the Scriptures. The Scriptures were written by men, but as they were "carried along by the Holy Spirit" (2 Peter 1 v 21). The Bible comes from God.

Help the group recognize that the Scriptures are not simply inspired by God (arising from him); rather, they are the very exhaling of God. The Scriptures have a divine origin; and God cannot lie (Titus 1 v 2). Men may err; confessions may err; creeds may err—but God cannot err, so the Scriptures are worthy of our trust above all else.

EXPLORE MORE
If the Scriptures are without error, then how do we explain errant teachings of the Scriptures or different interpretations of certain passages in the history of the church? Believing the Scriptures are without error does not mean that we believe all interpretations of Scripture are without error. Of course there will always be those whose hearts rebel against God's authority and his word, who will distort and seek to undermine Scripture. Even God-fearing, Bible-centered Christians can at times misunderstand, misconstrue, and misapply the Scriptures due to a lack of knowledge, or lack of application in learning God's word, or forgetfulness, or pursuit of one particular hobby horse. But the Scriptures themselves always remain without error.

What do the following passages indicate?
2 Corinthians 2 v 17; 4 v 2: Not all Bible teachers sincerely and faithfully teach God's truth; some use cunning or tamper with God's word for their own ends.

2 Timothy 4 v 3-4: Not all listeners want

to hear God's truth. People's desire to hear what they want to hear leads to an accumulation of errant teachers (v 3).

Hebrews 5 v 11-13: Some Christians don't grow in maturity, which leaves them "unskilled in the word of righteousness."

Romans 14 v 1-4, 17: There are some secondary matters on which Christians can hold different opinions.

1 Corinthians 13 v 9, 12: None of us will be perfect in knowledge until Christ returns, so we must remain humble.

9. How does Paul outline the sufficiency of the Scriptures in verses 16-17? When we truly believe that Scripture is sufficient for all of life and faith, we will use it for:

- teaching—sound instruction in the faith
- reproof—aimed at the conviction of a sinner
- correction—helping a sinner turn to truth
- training—growth in truth and godliness
- every good work—notice how all-encompassing (i.e. "sufficient") Paul's language is here

These attributes could easily apply to the entire life of salvation.

10. APPLY: In what ways does *Sola Scriptura* grant freedom to the Christian? Think about the Christian's confidence, authority and peace.
Confidence: The Christian doesn't need to wonder whether something else exists that they must know, believe, or understand.
Authority: Nothing can bind our conscience but the Scriptures alone. This prevents the Christian from being burdened by undue pressures, errant teachings and the dictates of others.
Peace: Whatever the circumstance, we possess an authoritative word from the Lord. God does not leave us alone to our own schemes, devising or doubts. He speaks into

our world with a clear and authoritative voice.

11. APPLY: From these two passages, what would you say to a person who says they have found a certain tradition helpful in their Christian life and they would like you to try it? God has spoken. His Scriptures are sufficient for salvation and the life of faith. Therefore, your question must be: is this tradition in agreement with the Scriptures? If not, we must readily reject it. No matter the perceived benefit this person may think they enjoy, it provides no value if it remains at odds with God's word. If it is in accord with God's word, then it may be worth exploring, though not essential. God's word alone is essential.

12. APPLY: In those times [when we do not properly desire to read, or value, the Scriptures] how can we encourage our love for the Scriptures? Allow the group to brainstorm many different disciplines and helps. Encourage them to speak from personal experience. Every Christian experiences "dry times" in the Christian faith. What did they find helpful in re-igniting a love for the Scriptures?

2
Isaiah 53 v 1-12; 1 John 2 v 1-2
SOLUS CHRISTUS: IN CHRIST ALONE

THE BIG IDEA
As our Savior and Mediator, Christ has accomplished the necessary work for our salvation completely.

SUMMARY
The temptation to add more to the finished work of Christ routinely arises as an errant teaching in church history. The Reformers rightly understood that adding anything to (or taking anything away from) the person and work of Christ as necessary for our salvation undermines that salvation. Christ's life and death sufficiently secured eternal life for his people, finally and completely. No works can be added, no indulgences (partial reductions of punishment for sins) can be bought, nor prayers offered to Mary or the saints that merit anything for our salvation. He alone is salvation for all those who place their faith in him.

Isaiah 53 is one of the great Messianic texts of the Old Testament, prophesying about this Savior who was to come and the salvation he would accomplish. He suffered in our place, as our substitute, bearing our iniquity, and now extends to us his righteousness. "With his wounds we are healed." There is no need for anything or anyone else.

1 John 2 v 1-2 underscores the importance of Christ as our Mediator. Before the throne of God the Father, the Righteous One pleads the merit of his blood for saved sinners. We have much assurance, hope, and comfort in such a Savior.

OPTIONAL EXTRA
(Following Questions 8 and 9 on 1 John 2 v 1-2) As a group, sing (or read the lyrics of) *Arise, My Soul, Arise* by Charles Wesley or *When I Survey the Wondrous Cross* by Isaac Watts. Talk through the meaning of each verse and how it proclaims the truths of these two passages.

GUIDANCE FOR QUESTIONS
1. Identify some symbols that you immediately recognize, and the organization or entity they represent. Examples may include:
- a red cross on a white background—signifies the Red Cross
- a yellow M—immediately identifies a restaurant as McDonald's
- a white apple with a bite taken out of the side—marks a device manufactured by Apple

Discuss why these signs or symbols became the identifying markers for these entities and why they prove to be recognizable. The cross often represents Christianity, and rightfully so. It is at the very center and heart of our faith.

2. What do verses 1-3 emphasize about Christ's life? Christ's humble circumstances are clearly seen in these verses. He lived a life of suffering. When we think of our suffering Savior, we tend to think only of his crown of thorns, the nails in his hands, and his body hanging on a cross. Yet our Lord suffered in countless ways for us. Help the group to think through the sufferings Christ endured even before the cross.

3. In verses 4-6, identify the singular pronouns / possessive adjectives (he, him, his) and the plural ones (our, we, us). What are the implications of how these are used? First, help the group see that in the passage Christ is alone, while "we" are not. He alone bore our griefs, carried our sorrows, was stricken, smitten by God, afflicted, etc. We are grouped together in all going astray and turning our own way—not one of us stands outside that category. Second, recognize that Christ's death was substitutionary. The griefs, sorrows, transgressions, and iniquities are not his; they are ours!

- **Why did Christ suffer these things?** There are two answers to this question from the text. First, he suffered for our sake (v 4, 5, 8, 11, 12). Second, he suffered because God willed it. The Lord "laid on him the iniquity of us all" (v 6; see also v 10).

4. In verse 11, what is highlighted about Christ? Why is he alone a worthy sacrifice once for all for sinners? (See also Hebrews 10 v 1-14.) Christ possessed both knowledge of what was needed and the righteousness to fulfill what was required. Whereas "all we like sheep have gone astray" (Isaiah 53 v 6), he alone was without sin. He willingly lived a life of righteousness in order that his righteousness might become our righteousness—he makes "many to be accounted righteous" (v 11).

5. How does Isaiah clearly express the sufficiency of Christ's substitutionary death for our salvation (v 4, 5, 11)? Christ deals with all the "griefs" and "sorrows" of our lives (v 4) and all our moral failures and sin ("transgressions" and

"iniquities", v 5). He brings healing (v 5) for the former and "peace" (v 5) for the latter. It is accomplished. He makes "many to be accounted righteous" (v 11).

EXPLORE MORE
Read Acts 8 v 26-35. How does this passage inform our interpretation and understanding of Isaiah 53? It's about Jesus—that's how Philip interpreted this passage from Isaiah.
How did reading Isaiah 53 lead to the very salvation of the Ethiopian eunuch? Philip pointed the Ethiopian eunuch to Christ and Christ alone. The eunuch encountered the good news about Jesus from this Scripture (v 35) and this resulted in his salvation (as evidenced by the sign of baptism). Christ is sufficient to save and the word reveals Christ to us.

6. APPLY: Why is it impossible for Christians to overemphasize the cross? Why would it be accurate to say there is no gospel without the cross? This is an opportunity for the group to reflect with awe, gratitude and joy on the wonder of the cross. Don't miss this opportunity! Consider pausing for a few minutes of prayer.

- **Can you think of any practices in the history of the church that have undermined the doctrine of the sufficiency of Christ's substitutionary death for sinners? How have they done this?** Examples may include penance (a self-inflicted punishment as a sign and act of repentance), indulgences (see Summary), prayers for the dead, prayer to Mary and the saints, purgatory (a place of limited punishment before entering heaven for sins committed), etc.

- **Why are these practices harmful? Why would they offend God?** People may derive much comfort from various religious practices, but it proves to be a false comfort. It leads people to trust in and rely upon something other than Christ, when God has appointed Christ alone as the sufficient and necessary Savior of mankind. Turning to or relying upon other things makes a mockery of the cross and the great sacrifice of our Savior.

⊗

- **In addition to the practices mentioned above, in what ways can Christ's substitutionary death for sinners be undermined or sidelined today?** You may feel that your group doesn't have sufficient knowledge of current doctrinal trends to enable them to usefully discuss this, but if they can understand the issues involved, this question may be helpful to show how the battle to preserve *Solus Christus* continues today. Help the group to see that undermining or sidelining Christ's substitutionary death for sinners can be quite subtle but it is incredibly damaging. For example:
  - Christ's death is presented as an example of self-sacrificing love—without any explanation of its purpose: to bear our sins and punishment.
  - Or baptism is considered essential for salvation—baptism is commanded by Christ and important, but it does not save. Christ alone saves. Baptism is a sign of his saving work.
  - Or outreach focuses on serving the community, campaigning for social justice or showing non-churchgoers how normal we are—without any proclamation of sin and judgment: the necessary context for grasping the greatness and necessity of Christ's salvation.

7. APPLY: How would you use this passage to challenge someone:
- **who thinks there are many ways to God?**
- **who believes their sin is so great that they must add good works to Christ's work?**

Split the small group into pairs. Assign half the pairs the first example and the other half the second example. Ask the pairs to make notes and report back to the larger group how they would use this passage to challenge someone who held to such a perspective.

8. What does John say is his purpose in writing (1 John 2 v 1)? John is concerned for the Christian and their life in Christ. He desires to see the Christian live in the full freedom of their new life free from sin.

- **Read Romans 7 v 15; Hebrews 12 v 1-4; James 5 v 16, 19-20. Do Christians sin?** Of course Christians sin. We know this not only from the Scriptures, but by experience. We are never free from sin in this life. John's point here, as elsewhere in the book (e.g. 1 John 3 v 9-10), is that a Christian is changed by the grace of God and the work of the Spirit so that they cannot live in a habitual pattern of sin.

9. What truth should comfort us when we do sin (v 1-2)? Christ, as our Savior, serves as our advocate and mediator (our go-between) with the Father. Jesus, as the God-man, reconciles God to man and man to God. He intercedes for us before the throne of God (see Romans 8 v 34).

- **What allows Christ alone to occupy this role? Why can no other individual occupy this role?** He is righteous (1 John 2 v 1) and has made propitiation (see "Dictionary") for our sins (v 2). No other individual in the history of humanity has been without sin (Romans 3 v 23). All have needed the saving work of Christ. He alone is the spotless lamb (1 Peter 1 v 19), able to atone for sin (bear the guilt of sinners and the condemnation we deserve) and plead the merit of his righteous life before the Father.

EXPLORE MORE
What do the following passages proclaim regarding Christ's role as our Mediator?
- **Romans 8 v 33-34:** There are plenty of accusations that can be brought against God's people, but we can be confident that none of them will result in our condemnation by God, not because we are without sin, but because Christ's death and intercession for us is sufficient to overrule all condemnation.
- **Hebrews 7 v 25**: Christ shall always live and in that living is always interceding for us.
- **1 Timothy 2 v 5:** Christ's identity—fully man as well as fully God—and Christ's work of giving himself as a ransom for all means that only he is uniquely qualified to intercede on man's behalf before God.

10. APPLY: Imagine a Christian who knows their past sins were atoned for in Christ, but struggles to believe that their most recent sins as a Christian are sufficiently provided for in Christ? How would you counsel them? We would endeavor to demonstrate the context of this passage and that John's very purpose in writing these words is to address Christians who have sinned. Christians sin, but we have One who is the propitiation for our sins—not just for some of our sins, but for all our sins. His atoning work was once for all and there is no need to supplement his work. In fact, even now, he intercedes for us before the throne of God.

- **What could this person see in your life that would help them believe the truth of your words about Christ's once-for-all atonement?**
  - That although we freely confess our sin, we are not fearful of God's condemnation.
  - That we are quick to confess sin and seek God's forgiveness.
  - That we find our primary source of comfort and joy in the message of the cross and in the One who died for us there.
  - That we are zealous in the struggle against sin.

11. APPLY: Why has there been a tendency in the history of the church to add to the work of Christ, do you think? Fallen human nature is proud. It leads us to attempt to secure our salvation rather than humbly receive that which is gifted to us. Christ crucified tends to be a stumbling block and a subject of folly (1 Corinthians 1 v 23) to fallen men and women. The Christian life begins with a recognition that we are sinners and have nothing to give, and that Christ is righteous and has all to give. It demands humility (Luke 18 v 9-14).

- **Why should we continue to emphasize and boldly proclaim the importance of the cross?** Without the cross we have no faith, no Savior, and no life—it is that essential. We abandon it not only to our harm, but to our death. As Christians, we know that Christ's life and substitutionary death upon the cross are the most important truths for every single human being who has or shall ever be.

3 Deuteronomy 7 v 6-8; 9 v 1-6; Ephesians 2 v 1-10

SOLA GRATIA:
BY GRACE ALONE

THE BIG IDEA

Salvation is by grace alone. We all are sinners, who cannot and will not contribute anything to our salvation. Our salvation is accomplished by the sovereign unmerited favor of God, who freely chooses to save sinners.

SUMMARY

The issue in the Reformation was not whether we are saved by grace, through faith, in Christ. Everyone agreed with these principles. The issue was whether we are saved by grace *alone*, through faith *alone*, in Christ *alone*. *Alone* makes all the difference. Grace alone emphasizes the essential truth that our salvation is wholly of the Lord. He ordains, provides, accomplishes and secures it. Salvation is wholly by his grace and his grace alone. As sinners, we are unable to come to him or offer anything to him. Furthermore, God is not obligated to save sinners. He is not coerced, forced, manipulated or cajoled into saving sinners. Our salvation is by his own sovereign free choice. He extends unmerited favor (grace) to sinners in desperate need.

Christianity's teaching that salvation is wholly an act of God's sovereign free grace differentiates the Christian faith from all other world religions. We could not and did not choose him; he chose us. Salvation is not realized in seeking for, aspiring, climbing or ascending to heaven; it is realized by his grace flowing down. This is the message of the Scriptures in both the Old and New Testaments.

Deuteronomy 7 v 6-8 gives a clear articulation of this truth in the Old Testament. It clearly asserts why God chose to save Israel out of all the nations on the face of the earth. Deuteronomy 9 v 1-6 serves as a reminder of how great God's saving grace is. In Ephesians 2 v 1-10, Paul underscores the state of all human beings prior to being saved in Christ, and then proclaims the beauty of God's saving grace in light of our destitute condition.

OPTIONAL EXTRA

Find the website of a dog re-homing charity from which you can download and print out images and profiles of different dogs that need a new owner. Pass these around your group and get them to choose the one that they would most like to take home. Ask people to explain their choice e.g. because of looks, size, age, hairiness, temperament, amount of exercise needed, past history, etc. Are there dogs that no one wants? After question 3 you could compare the group's choices with God's choice of his people—based not on any attractive or desirable characteristics, for no one has anything attractive or desirable to offer God, but purely on his free grace.

GUIDANCE FOR QUESTIONS

1. What is the best gift you have received (e.g. birthday, wedding, anniversary, Mother's Day, etc.)? Use this time to reflect upon the reason why these gifts were special. No doubt they conveyed love—maybe from a spouse, daughter, son or friend. What makes gifts special is that they can only be received. They are undeserved. We cannot earn gifts or else they cease to be gifts, so they often convey the love of another in significant ways.

2. What does it mean that God chose Israel out of all the peoples on the face of the earth (7 v 6)? He chose them to be his people and the objects of his saving work. He showed them his favor.

- **Note that they did not choose God: God chose them. Why is this important?** Because their relationship with God was not the fruit of their desires, willingness or efforts; it was an act of God. Apart from his choice, they would have been listed with the likes of the Hittites, Girgashites, Amorites, Canaanites, Perizzites, Hivites, and Jebusites of verse 1. (See that God also chose us in relation to our New Testament passage, Ephesians 1 v 4-5.)

3. Why were they alone of "all the peoples who are on the face of the earth" counted as "his treasured possession" and shown favor (v 7-8)? It was not because of who they were (i.e. "more in number than any other people"), what they had done (note that they had just wandered in the wilderness for forty years due to rebelliousness and disobedience; see Numbers 32 v 13), or who they would be. (Israel's story in the Old Testament is one of continual disobedience). The Lord counted Israel has his treasured possession and chose to show them his favor and save them out of sheer love—an undeserved love: grace.

- **Where had God acted in the same way previously in Bible history?** (If people don't know much Bible history, you could briefly take them through a couple of the events outlined here.) His choosing to make Abraham into a great nation (see Genesis 15) was also an act of grace, as was continuing the promise through Isaac instead of Ishmael (see Genesis 21), and favoring Jacob over Esau (see Genesis 25; Romans 9). God saves those he loves and loves those he saves. Throughout history God demonstrates that his people are his people by grace.

4. What did Moses remind the people of? What did he warn them against? Why is this important in the context? Moses reminded them of their rebelliousness and he warned against pride. As they were about to enter the land and destroy the pagan nations, the temptation to think that they were morally superior and deserving would be great. Moses reminds the nation of their own sinfulness and warns them against such arrogance, so they might be quick to give thanksgiving to God and give him glory for his great grace and covenant love. As much as these nations were the recipients of God's wrath, so the Israelites were the recipients of his grace. God sovereignly chose to respond to the nations' sins with justice and Israel's sins with grace. He could have chosen to do differently. It was nothing that he saw in Israel that led him to dispense such kindness, but rather it was an act of sheer grace.

5. APPLY: What practical importance does God's free, sovereign choice to save people by an act of gracious love have upon our preaching, teaching, and evangelizing as Christians? The answers elicited from your group could be many. Examples may include: humility must mark our ministries—we are never the primary cause for anything good happening; prayer to a sovereign God saturates our preaching;

no one is to be considered too sinful for us to share the good news of God's grace with them subject; we seek to use God's means (the word and prayer) in reaching others for Christ.

6. What does Paul say about our condition before salvation (v 1-3)? We were dead in our sins (v 1, 5), following the world (v 2), enslaved to the devil (v 2), controlled by our flesh (v 3), and objects of the wrath of God (v 3).

- **Is this only true concerning some people? Why or why not?** All people are born into this world in such a condition. Paul employs inclusive language—"all once lived" (v 3) and "like the rest of mankind" (v 3). This is the doctrine of original sin. Due to Adam's sin in the garden of Eden (Genesis 3), everyone born into this world by natural generation is by nature a child of wrath (v 3). Sin is our nature (see also Romans 5 v 12-21)

7. What are the implications of being "*dead* in [our] trespasses and sins"? Help the group to think through the imagery of a corpse. A corpse lacks life, ability, will, or desire. We were a corpse spiritually— unable in any way to reach out to God. It required something outside of, apart from, and greater than, ourselves. Strive to help the members of the study understand our destitute, doomed, and deadly state apart from God's grace. We could not do anything about our state. We had nothing to offer.

EXPLORE MORE
Look at the following passages. What does each tell us about the state of fallen people?
John 3 v 19-20: Lovers of darkness, workers of evil deeds, haters of the light.
John 8 v 34: Slaves to sin.

Romans 3 v 10-18: Lacking righteousness, ignorant, not seeking God, not doing good, without any fear of God.
Romans 8 v 6-8: Hostile to God, not subject to the law of God, unable to be subject, cannot please God.
Colossians 3 v 5-7: Walking in sins for which the wrath of God is coming.

8. "Of course God will save; it is his job!" What is the problem with such a statement? We are sinners. He is wholly righteous and just. The sinner does not deserve salvation; rather, as sinners we deserve wrath—the wrath of a holy and just God. Yet, he bestows grace—an unmerited favor/love. You cannot deserve that which is unmerited. By definition, he cannot be required to give that which is undeserved and necessarily free. Truly, how amazing his grace is to sinners.

9. Why is it important to understand the depth of our sin and the wretchedness of our condition apart from Christ to truly value our salvation fully? The more we understand our sinfulness, the more we grasp the infinite beauty of this holy and righteous God's grace to us. The sinfulness of sin requires an abundant and sparkling grace.

10. Who is the active party in verses 4-7? God ("But God…" v 4)

- **What did God accomplish for us (v 5-8)?** God takes spiritually dead people and gives them life (v 5), raises them up with Christ—which implies forgiveness of sins and freedom from bondage to the world, the devil, and the flesh (v 3)—and seats them with Christ in the heavenly realm (v 6). He saves them.

- **Why did God choose to save us (v 4)?**

God chose to act according to his rich mercy (v 4). His great love for us (v 4; see also Ephesians 1 v 4-5), not our love for him, compelled him to save. This rich, merciful love bestowed upon sinners is grace—unmerited favor. As sinners, we are trapped in a miserable and deadly condition, but God sent his only Son into this world to live and die for sinners such as us.

- **How did God choose to save us (v 8)?** He saved us by grace. Paul underscores multiple times in this short passage the truth that God chose by his sovereign, free good pleasure to save sinners (see v 4—God being "rich in mercy," and "because of the great love with which he loved us"; v 7—that "he might show the immeasurable riches of his grace in kindness toward us"; v 8—"it is the gift of God").

11. Why should the doctrine of *Sola Gratia* put a stop to all boasting (v 9)? We were bought with a price (1 Corinthians 6 v 20), but not a price we could pay. No, we incurred a debt that left us destitute. Someone else had to purchase us. Our works could not merit our salvation. Notice that Paul emphatically points out this truth in v 8-9, both positively ("by grace" and "it is the gift of God", v 8) and negatively ("not your own doing," v 8 and "not a result of works," v 9). Our salvation had to be accomplished by Christ's work alone. It is his merit that secures salvation, not our own. It is his righteousness that satisfies the justice of God, not our own. It is his death that paid the penalty, not our own. Our salvation is a gift: nothing can be added to it, so any degree of boasting—no matter how small—has no place in the Christian's life (see 1 Corinthians 4 v 7). Grace by its very definition is undeserved.

12. APPLY: What would you say to the individual who believes "grace alone" undermines living a life of holiness to the Lord? Paul believes that grace leads to good works (v 10). These works do not merit salvation but are in response to salvation. "If you love me, you will keep my commandments," said Jesus (John 14 v 15). Why? Because grace begets gratitude. When we know what our lives have been saved from, it leads us to give thanksgiving with our lives to the One who saved us.

- **What characteristics would you expect to see in the life of someone who has grasped the truth that salvation comes to us by grace alone?** This question is an opportunity for people to summarize what they have learned about how *Sola Gratia* affects the way we live. Characteristics should include: gratitude to God, love for God, joy, humility, faithful obedience to Christ, serving and doing good in response to God's grace, lack of self-righteousness, free admission of sinfulness, sorrow over sin, lack of judgmentalism, and a desire to share the good news with all.

4 Psalm 32 v 1-11; Romans 3 v 21-26

SOLA FIDE:
THROUGH FAITH ALONE

THE BIG IDEA

Our justification (our right standing before God) is by faith alone. We are counted and declared just by the holy God due to a righteousness that is not our own, but granted to us and received by faith alone. Faith (receiving and resting on Christ and his righteousness) is the only instrument of (or, the only means by which we can receive) justification.

SUMMARY

In many ways the Reformation could be described as a movement to reassert the biblical doctrine of justification by faith alone. The Reformers called justification by faith the "material cause" of the Reformation because it involves the very material or substance of the gospel—what an individual must believe to be saved. Justification is by grace alone in Christ alone through faith alone. Our justification is not based upon merit. The holy God will never be satisfied with the works of fallen men. Neither is our justification based upon the infusion of Christ's righteousness in us (his righteousness growing in us and becoming our righteousness). Rather, our salvation is solely based upon the person of Christ and his righteousness, which is imputed (credited) to us and received by faith alone.

Psalm 32 asserts this truth by teaching the sinner to turn to God in faith. This psalm is labeled as "A Maskil of David." *Maskil* refers to a teaching. Most likely, David composed Psalm 32 in connection with Psalm 51.

Both of these psalms were written after David's sin with Bathsheba (2 Samuel 11). Psalm 32 may be David's fulfillment of his promise in Psalm 51 v 13, "Then I will teach transgressors your ways, and sinners will return to you." Clearly, Psalm 32 teaches the sinner that he/she can only be saved from the burden and weight of sin by turning to the Lord in faith.

In Romans 3 v 21-26 the apostle Paul clearly teaches this same salvation by faith alone. He underscores the Scripture's teaching that salvation is by grace through Christ's redeeming work and this gift can only be received by faith.

OPTIONAL EXTRA

Select three people in your group to participate in a competition. Promise a desirable prize for the winner. Each person will be given thirty seconds to catch as many balls as you throw at them. The first should be given a ball cap and told that they can only catch the balls in the cap. The second might be given a glass or another object which would make it impossible to accomplish the task. Ensure that neither of these individuals is able to catch a ball. Hand the third contestant a laundry basket with which they can catch the balls. Clearly, the third person should win the competition. When the complaints die down, ask the group why this individual so easily won the blessing. The answer is that they clearly had the instrument to receive the blessing. This lesson will focus on the truth that faith alone is the instrument by which we receive justification in Christ.

GUIDANCE FOR QUESTIONS

1. List some popular movies, television shows, and books that involve a courtroom scene or extended trials, and share your favorite. What makes this genre of entertainment stimulating for so many people? The answers could be numerous. Many courtroom scenes are high on drama because they deal with life-and-death issues. Furthermore, they contain many elements that stir human emotion: authority, justice, truth, righteousness, judgment, law, intrigue, guilt, forgiveness, etc. Point out that justification by faith alone has judicial overtones and is an eternal life-or-death issue.

2. What two aspects of salvation does David highlight in verse 1? Forgiveness—removing the guilt and offense. Covering—concealing what is still present.

3. What marks the "blessed" person? What does David mean by "blessed" (v 1-2)? The blessed person is one whose sins have been forgiven. David knows this blessing (see v 5) and desires others to experience it. "Blessed" could be interpreted as "happy." True happiness and freedom come in the actual forgiveness of sins—in being one "against whom the LORD counts no iniquity" (v 2).

- **How does this view of the "blessed" or "happy" person contrast with the world's view of the "happy" person?** We know true happiness when we are in restored life-giving, loving communion with God. The world promises happiness apart from God and promotes waywardness from his path. However, the world's happiness is fleeting, its joys are shallow, and its promises are ultimately empty.

4. Summarize David's transgressions (see 2 Samuel 11). Why did David feel as though his bones were wasting away, do you think (Psalm 32 v 3)? David committed grievous sin against the Lord (see Psalm 51 v 4). Sin disrupts our relationship with the living God and it burdens the conscience, making life laborious. Though David grieved for the suffering his sin incurred, as seen by his "groaning," he did not grieve for his actual sin against God (Psalm 32 v 3). As long as he refused to come to the Lord in confession, the burden of carrying the weight of this guilt made him feel as though the strongest parts of his body (i.e. his bones) would melt under the pressure.

Notice that David has come to understand that God sent him this experience of suffering ("your hand was heavy upon me," v 4). It is part of God's kindness to us that he doesn't allow his people to live at ease when there is sin in our lives that we have not repented of.

- **How did David eventually find relief and peace (v 5, 10)?** David confessed his sin and the Lord forgave (v 5). He trusted in the Lord and surrendered his burden to him (v 10). David turned to the Lord in faith.

- **Was David still a sinner when he found this relief? How do we know?** Yes, he remained a sinner. David says he is blessed because the Lord did not count his iniquity against him (v 2). David still had iniquity, but God no longer held it to his account. God covered his sins (v 1). We are not forgiven because we become righteous: we are forgiven and declared righteous. God forgave David because he trusted in him (v 10) and confessed his sin to him (v 5). David remained a sinner, but a sinner who exercised faith by turning to the Lord in trust.

EXPLORE MORE
Read Psalm 51. Compare Psalm 51 to Psalm 32. Look for similar terms (e.g. transgressions, sin) and themes (e.g. forgiveness, the weight of guilt). What truths here do you think might surprise someone who doesn't know the message of the Bible? Answers might include: v 1—that God's mercy is abundant; v 2—that we can be thoroughly cleansed from our sin; v 4—that sin is primarily against God; v 5—that we are sinful from our conception; v 8—that God "breaks our bones" when our sin is unconfessed.

5. APPLY: From personal experience, what are some of the benefits you as a Christian enjoy by confessing your sins to God? Allow the group to range in answer to the question as it will benefit the entire group. Prepare something to say yourself in case people are slow to talk. Some of the answers you want to be sure to bring to the forefront are that confession reminds us of the holiness of God, reorients our thinking from self to God, directs our affections to Christ, relieves the burden of guilt, strengthens us for resisting temptation in the future, and provides peace of conscience.

6. Why does Paul say that the "righteousness of God" has been manifested (shown) now (3 v 21)? God fully manifests his saving righteousness in this age of salvation history—after Jesus—through the life, death and resurrection of Christ. God has always saved sinful people in the same way, through faith in Christ (the Old Testament believer looked forward to Christ), but now that Christ has come, the righteousness of God in the person of Christ has been fully revealed.

• **Salvation through faith in Christ was not a new idea in salvation history (v 21-22). Why is this essential to understand?** The Law and the Prophets (i.e. Old Testament Scriptures) bore witness to this being the way of salvation. If faith in Christ was a new way of salvation, there would be an Old Testament path and a New Testament path. This would mean the Bible presents two ways of salvation. Paul clearly articulates in this passage that faith in Christ has always been the way of salvation, both in the Old Testament and New Testament eras.

⌄

• **Read Romans 4 v 1-12. Paul highlights Abraham and circumcision when discussing the necessity of faith for salvation. How does Paul's argument in this passage confirm that salvation in both the Old and New Testaments was by faith alone?** Paul takes the great person of the Old Testament (Abraham) and the great sign performed by the saints of the Old Testament (circumcision) and highlights the truth that God justified Abraham before he was circumcised. Obedience to the law did not justify Abraham. Rather, he was justified by faith. Obedience to the law came in response to being justified. Abraham was saved by grace through faith, not works. (Note John 8 v 56—Abraham looked forward to Christ.)

7. Why is it impossible for people to be saved through their law-keeping (v 21, 23)? Why must the righteousness we

need come from outside us? Point out Romans 3 v 10-12 to the group. All have turned aside and no one does good (v 12). The Bible couldn't be clearer. Help the group to see that all people are sinners and no one keeps the law (v 23). In fact, we are all in the helpless state that David confessed in Psalm 32. The weight of sin and guilt lay heavy upon us and there is no work we can do to relieve the burden. Perfect righteousness remains the standard of the Law and we are unable to meet it. People need righteousness from outside of ourselves, a righteousness that is not our own. And this God provides as we receive the very "righteousness of God" (v 22) by faith.

8. Why was it necessary for salvation that there should be a propitiatory sacrifice (v 25)? (You might want to remind people of the definition of "propitiation." See "Dictionary" on p27.)
1. The holy God must uphold justice.
2. Justice requires that wrongdoing must be punished, because wrongdoing harms or takes from its victim. Punishment is what restores equilibrium between the wrongdoer and the wronged victim (think of how justice is often represented by a set of scales which are level).
3. So God cannot uphold perfect justice without punishing every wrong that has been committed. That's why v 25 raises the "problem" of God passing over former sins. Until Jesus' death on the cross, there had been no sufficient penalty paid for every sin committed by humans. In fact, each and every new animal sacrifice demonstrated that no mere animal sacrifice could atone for all human sin.
4. God put forward Jesus as a "propitiation by his blood" (v 25)—that is, his death was able to pay the penalty that human sins deserved, because he was fully human. It

was also sufficient due to his infinite worth as being fully God. God's justice and wrath are satisfied by the death of Jesus, the God-man.
5. Jesus' death shows God's righteousness (v 25, 26) because it has overcome the apparent problem of God's forbearance of sin (v 25). God's right and just wrath needed to be satisfied or God would cease to be who he is—the perfectly holy and just God.

- **How does the death of Jesus on the cross satisfy this need (v 26)?** God has become both the just and the justifier. He who is perfectly holy, the Son of God, has maintained the righteous standard of God's law by living a perfectly holy life as a human. He then satisfied the demands of the law against sinners by taking the place of sinners and himself suffering the penalty we deserve in bearing the wrath of God on the cross and being subjected to death. The claims of the law have been fully satisfied by his perfect life and sacrifice; the standard has been met and justice has been upheld.

- **Some opponents of the gospel argue that the righteous Christ taking the place of sinners and bearing their penalty makes a mockery of law and justice. Why is that not the case?** The law has not been suspended or undone. Christ upholds the law. In fact, it has been fulfilled. The requirements of the law were satisfied as Christ took our place upon the cross.

Note: *Imputed righteousness v Infused righteousness.* Both the Roman Catholic Church and the Reformers believed that an individual was justified by faith. Once again, as we have seen with the other *Solas,* the issue of contention centered around the word "alone." In addition, there was disagreement about the meaning of justification itself. Is our justification founded upon the righteousness of Christ imputed (credited) to us or the righteousness of Christ working within us?

The Reformers rightly understood that Christ's righteousness is imputed to the sinner and that God declares us righteous by virtue of that gracious act of imputation. God does not declare us righteous because we bear the signs of innocence, but rather, because a righteousness that is not our own is reckoned to us when the Holy Spirit unites us to Christ by faith. Yet, it is a real righteousness, because it is a real imputation that occurs within a real Spirit-wrought union with the righteous Christ. Note that this is a legal/courtroom declaration. It is an act of God that coincides with the moment a Christian exercises the gift of faith; it is not a process.

By contrast, the Roman Catholic Church teaches that Christ's righteousness is infused in the sinner, thus becoming part of his/her person, progressively and inwardly renovating a person's heart. This view holds that a person is not *declared* righteous, but *becomes* righteous. This process is said to begin at baptism with the infusion of Christ's righteousness, and to progress as an individual merits their salvation by continuing in this grace through living a moral life, doing good works, and practicing religious rituals.

9. What role does faith play in our salvation (v 25-26)? We do not *do* to gain justification, but rather, we *believe*. Faith has often been referred to as the instrument of our justification. It is the means by which we receive the righteousness of God in Christ Jesus.

• **How would you reply to someone who says that faith is a work (that is, it's something we do that *merits* salvation) (v 24)?** Faith cannot be a work; it is a gift (v 24; also see Ephesians 2 v 8). Faith receives and in this sense is passive. Faith is simply resting in Christ Jesus. We are not saved by the act of believing, but by the finished work of Christ and trusting in him. You might share with your group the quote from B.B. Warfield, a 19th-century Princeton theologian, who said, "The saving power of faith resides thus not in itself, but in the Almighty Savior on whom it rests … It is not strictly speaking, even faith in Christ that saves, but Christ that saves through faith."

EXPLORE MORE
Read Romans 10 v 14-17. Identify and discuss each use of the word "belief" or "faith" here.
What practical implications does this text have for: • the church? • the individual Christian? • your family?
"Faith comes from hearing … the word of Christ" (v 17), so we must preach the good news and send those who will preach the good news. Get people to share how this might apply to their churches, themselves and their families.

10. APPLY: How would you explain saving faith to an individual who believes that general faith in God saves, and that one doesn't necessarily need to believe in Christ? Faith in God is insufficient. It is essential that we communicate to others that they must place their faith in *Christ* to be saved. Jesus said, "I am the way, and the truth, and the life. No one comes to the Father except through me" (John 14 v 6). There is no way to God apart from Christ. We must receive Christ and rest in him alone for our salvation.

11. APPLY: Martin Luther, the Reformer, said, "If the article [doctrine] of justification is lost, all Christian doctrine is lost at the same time." Why is he correct? Justification is the very heart of the gospel. When the biblical doctrine of justification is denied, every other doctrine falls with it. Get people to think about what wrong beliefs emerge when the teaching of justification through faith in Christ is rejected. Here are just a few examples: our eyes are taken off of Christ; Christ's substitutionary sacrifice is undervalued; Christ's perfect righteousness diminishes in importance; grace evaporates; works or sentimentalism quickly replace faith; the sacraments (baptism and the Lord's Supper) are misunderstood; sanctification (growing in holiness) becomes a means of securing God's favor; eternal security is lost, etc.

12. APPLY: What comforts should mark the life of an individual who knows that they are justified by grace alone in Christ alone through faith alone? Get people to think from their own experience of how understanding and trusting in this teaching has brought them comfort and joy. They should be "happy" (Psalm 32) in Christ, not fear condemnation, know freedom from guilt, be confident in their eternal security, desire to honor God with a life of thanksgiving, delight in Christ, long to grow in faith and faithfulness, etc.

Psalms 19 v 12; 24 v 1-2; Romans 11 v 33 – 12 v 2

5 SOLI DEO GLORIA: GLORY TO GOD ALONE

THE BIG IDEA
All glory is due to God alone. He created all things, sustains all things, and is the goal of all things. This means that he alone is also due all glory for our salvation as it was appointed by him, accomplished by him and ultimately has his glory as its goal.

SUMMARY
The Reformers greatly concerned themselves with trumpeting the biblical teaching that all things exist for the glory of God. They proclaimed the teaching of Scripture that God remains jealous for his own glory; he will not share it with another. Therefore, the Reformers rightly understood that all the other *Solas* of the Reformation had as their aim the very glory of God. Scripture alone, grace alone, Christ alone, and faith alone all point to the fact that our salvation (and all of life) is for the glory of God alone.

This *Sola* serves as the great unifier of all these doctrines. In addition, the Reformers helped to bring to light once again that according to the Scriptures, people always live before the face of God and must labor to live to the glory of God. His glory shapes our work, play, worship, family—all of life.

In Psalm 19 v 1-2 we see that all creation speaks of its Creator. Psalm 24 v 1-2 spells out the implication that all things exist for the glory of this Creator God. This is our starting place. Even before we look at our salvation giving glory to God, it is helpful to recognize that everything exists for the glory of God. Therefore, it does not surprise us to learn that our salvation also aims at this goal. Romans 11 v 33-36 will highlight this truth as Paul exclaims in doxology. The final two verses, Romans 12 v 1-2, orient the Christian to living a life to the glory of God.

OPTIONAL EXTRA

Find out some facts about the universe (e.g. How many stars are there? How big is the largest known star? How far is the nearest star? How long would it take to get there? How big is the sun? How many galaxies do we know of? How fast do comets travel? How far is the furthest star we know of? How quickly is the universe expanding? How much of the universe can we see?) Slowly read out each fact, or get people in your group to do this. Then discuss how people feel when they look at the night sky and think about space. (Links with the first passage in this study, which tells us that the sky reveals the glory of God; see Q2.)

GUIDANCE FOR QUESTIONS

1. What are some different pursuits and goals that shape people's lives? This study explores the practical implications that the glory of God has upon the Christian life. He is to shape our living and his glory is to be our pursuit.

2. What does David mean when he says, "The heavens declare the glory of God" and, "The sky above proclaims his handiwork" (v 1)? God's person is revealed when we look up at the sky by day and night. Each directs our attention to him.

• **How do the day and night skies declare the glory of God and proclaim**

his handiwork? Give time for the group to brainstorm and reflect. This exercise should encourage and stimulate. As the discussion leader, you may eventually want to take the group to Romans 1 v 19-20 and lead them through a discussion of the attributes of God that are reflected and revealed in nature (e.g. a thunderstorm points to his power, the endless night sky points to his infinitude, a garden to his beauty, etc.).

• **What is the importance of the repetition in "day to day" and "night to night" (v 2)?** Day and night continue to come. There is an unbroken cycle. The witness to God in creation never ceases. People have a reminder day in and day out, night in and night out, of the glory and majesty of God.

3. Why is it fitting that all creation should exist to bring glory to God (Psalm 24 v 1-2)? Because he is the Creator of the earth. God created all things out of nothing by the word of his power in Genesis 1 and 2. He deserves praise for making something of such wonder, beauty and order.

• **What is the implication the psalmist derives from God creating all things (Psalm 24 v 1)?** The earth and all that fills it belongs to the Lord. Note that "those who dwell" in it also belong to the Lord. All of creation was created for and to him (his glory is the goal of all creation), including each of us. We tend to think and live as if the world was created for us, but this is not the case. Since he is the Creator, all of creation was created for his purposes and aimed at his glory.

EXPLORE MORE
Read Psalm 19 v 1-14. How else does

the Lord reveal himself and what is significant about this? The Lord reveals himself through his word. Discuss the difference between God's revelation through nature and his revelation through Scripture. Nature reveals that God exists and generally reveals some of his attributes, which is enough to condemn all people (see Romans 1 v 19-20). Theologians label this "general revelation." Scripture reveals more clearly who God is, his will, and what is necessary for salvation and life. The Scriptures constitute what theologians term "special revelation."

4. APPLY: What is the practical significance of everything being created for the glory of God? How does this impact your life? First and foremost, it means that God alone deserves our worship. Everything else has been created for his glory. Therefore anything and everyone else that we would glorify or worship instead of God is an idol, which the Bible describes as evil, worthless, detestable and an abomination that provokes him to anger. Second, it means my life is a life that is to be lived in worship. As Paul said to the Corinthians, "Whether you eat or drink, or whatever you do, do all to the glory of God" (1 Corinthians 10 v 31).

5. Typically, when we don't understand something completely, it makes us uneasy and anxious. Yet Paul highlights the depths of God's wisdom and knowledge, the unsearchableness of his judgments, and the inscrutability of his ways, and instead of causing him anxiety, it leads him to praise. Why is this, do you think? Though it rightfully induces fear (Proverbs 1 v 7), knowing that a being exists who is very unlike us—knowing all things, directing all things to their best

end, having knowledge that we do not possess, and operating in ways that we don't understand—also provides comfort. He is this great, and yet equally good—choosing to redeem and save otherwise hopeless sinners. We do not glory in God until we have reckoned with our own lack of glory.

6. Why is it significant in relation to our salvation that no one has served as the Lord's counselor (v 34)? No one possesses superior wisdom or knowledge to that which God possesses. Our salvation was not the result of the counsel of angels, the pleadings of men, or some other scheme. Our salvation was decreed in the eternal counsels of the triune Godhead; it was his will and his desire alone. This reveals his unparalleled and inconceivably wonderful love (see 1 John 4 v 10), and the only fitting response is to say, "To him be glory forever" (Romans 11 v 36).

- **Why is it significant in relation to our salvation that no one "has given a gift to him that he might be repaid" (v 35)?** God is never a debtor. No person can place God under obligation to give anything, let alone salvation. So no one can take any of the glory for anyone's salvation. Rather, our salvation is wholly by his grace, giving us all the more reason to ascribe to him the glory that is due his name (Psalm 29 v 2).

7. How does verse 36 echo the theology we observed in Psalms 19 and 24? All things, meaning the totality of the universe, come "from him"—he created it all. All things are also "through him"—he sustains them all. Furthermore, all things are "to him"—he is the goal of all. He is the Creator, the Sustainer, and the Goal of all things.

- **How does this inform our understanding of the purpose of salvation?** Note that in this context, the "all" includes our salvation. Our salvation gives God glory. In fact, this is the primary purpose in God decreeing and accomplishing salvation for his elect (the people he has chosen to save). Of course, we are the beneficiaries of this salvation, but we are saved "to the praise of his glorious grace" (Ephesians 1 v 6). God determined it, accomplished it, and is the ultimate goal of it. Therefore, Paul finds his mind and heart filled with thanksgiving and praise to God for this unbelievable salvation, and rightfully so. In essence, God's accomplishment of our salvation is his glory (that which eternally and inherently marks him) revealed outwardly.

8. What [does Romans 12 v 1-2] indicate about the connection between Romans 1 – 11 and the rest of Paul's letter? Paul is arguing that the great salvation that he has outlined should impel us to respond by offering our bodies as living sacrifices, which means we will no longer live like the world but will be transformed in our minds so that we can live God's way. From this we can see that doctrine gives rise to living. For instance, justification (understanding that in Christ God has declared me holy) necessitates sanctification (now I seek to grow in holiness). And grace (understanding that I have been saved because of God's undeserved kindness and not through any obedience of mine) leads to obedience.

EXPLORE MORE
Briefly skim Romans 12 – 16. What are some of the instructions Paul gives for living to the glory of God?
Examples:
- "Abhor what is evil; hold fast to what is good" (12 v 9).
- "Love one another with brotherly affection" (12 v 10).
- "Repay no one evil for evil, but give thought to do what is honorable in the sight of all" (12 v 17).
- "Pay to all what is owed to them: taxes to whom taxes are owed, revenue to whom revenue is owed, respect to whom respect is owed, honor to whom honor is owed" (13 v 7).
- "Let us not pass judgment on one another any longer, but rather decide never to put a stumbling block or hindrance in the way of a brother" (14 v 13).
- "Welcome one another as Christ has welcomed you, for the glory of God" (15 v 7).
- "Watch out for those who cause divisions and create obstacles contrary to the doctrine that you have been taught; avoid them" (16 v 17).

9. It is essential to understand that *Soli Deo Gloria* (glory to God alone) is first about God's glory rather than about us giving him glory. Why, do you think? This proves to be a fine distinction, but a necessary distinction. If we primarily understand this *Sola* as referring to the call upon Christians to live to the glory of God, then, ironically, we make *Soli Deo Gloria* focus on us rather than God. This doctrine becomes people-centered instead of God-centered. *Soli Deo Gloria* is first and foremost about God, who has all glory. We add nothing to him; no one gives a gift to him that he might be repaid (11 v 35). All glory is his. Once we understand that truth, then we can encourage Christians to rightfully ascribe to him the glory that is due his name (Psalm 29 v 2) by living to his glory. We ascribe it to him because it is already his. We give him glory because he is glorious, and gloriously accomplished our salvation.

10. Why would Paul say that glory should be given to God "forever" (11 v 36)?
1. God's saving work is so great that it should elicit praise for all eternity.
2. Our salvation lasts forever, so his praise should extend forever.
3. God is eternal, so the glory that is given to such a great God must be eternal.
4. He is worthy! (Also note that "glory" in v 36 is preceded by an article—"the"—in the original Greek. Verse 36 literally says, "To him be the glory forever. Amen." God alone is deserving of the glory that lasts forever and ever.)

11. APPLY: All things are for the glory of God. In what ways should this affect our lives in the following areas?
• Marriage • Parenting • Recreation • Finances • Worship • Work
Press the group to "dig deep." This question could challenge and encourage the members of the study in wonderful ways, but only if they are willing to go beyond the superficial.

12. APPLY: How do all the other *Solas* (Scripture alone, Christ alone, grace alone, and faith alone) lead to this final *Sola*? Give the group some silent time to jot down their thoughts to this question and then ask them to share these ideas with the rest of the group.
All the *Solas* exalt and glorify God. Our salvation is by grace alone in Christ alone through faith alone, without any meritorious work on our part; therefore all the glory belongs to God for our salvation, not to us. It comes from him, is through him, and is to him.
Scripture: It is from God alone (inspired) and leads to God alone.
Christ: He is from God, is God, and points to God.
Grace: It flows from God and comes only through the work of God.
Faith: It is a gift from God that unites a person to God.

Psalm 78; 2 Timothy 1 v 1-14

6 PRESERVING AND PRESSING ON

THE BIG IDEA
God entrusts Christians with the faith. Each of us bears responsibility individually and corporately to preserve and pass on this faith to the following generation.

SUMMARY
This study series examined the five *Solas* of the Reformation from the Scriptures.

As we have seen, these doctrines are not tangential, but encompass the very heart of the gospel. Therefore, we cannot and must not lose these doctrines that are crucial, not just for the Reformation but for our Christian faith. It is incumbent upon each generation to preserve and pass on this faith to the generation which follows.

This final study looks at two key passages

in the Scriptures which highlight this need for believers to hold on to the faith and teach the following generation. Psalm 78 demonstrates this emphasis in the Old Testament and Paul's words to Timothy in 2 Timothy show this necessity in the New Testament. Though the writings were aimed at different audiences, they have the same message—preserve and pass on the one true faith. Every generation receives this charge; we are no different.

OPTIONAL EXTRA

As an ice-breaker, you could bring a few different items from home. Some of the items should be meaningless, while others hold significance for you and your family. Show each item to the group and ask them whether they think the item is meaningful or not so meaningful to your family. Ask how they came to those conclusions. Explain why the meaningful pieces are meaningful for you. This exercise easily leads into the first question.

GUIDANCE FOR QUESTIONS

1. What is your family's greatest possession? If it is old, how many generations passed it down through your family? Why is this heirloom important to your family? In these passages we will see the greatest gift of our lives. Psalm 78 and 2 Timothy 1 highlight the great gift of God that the previous generations have entrusted to us: the one true faith.

2. What does Asaph want the people to pay attention to (v 1-3)? There is knowledge he wants them to hear and understand. This knowledge involves the history of the nation of Israel. He calls it "dark sayings," not because the information is evil, but because history by itself is a kind

of tangled mess. It requires interpretation or making sense of. He wants them to listen to this history intently and understand the message it conveys.

- **What is the central theme he wants them to see in this history (v 4)?** The glorious deeds of the LORD and his might are the focus of Asaph's story. Yes, it is a history of the nation of Israel, but it only makes sense through the eyes of faith. And Asaph wants his listeners to know this history of God willing and working for the redemption of his people. There is much to learn here for the people of faith.

3. What responsibility and privilege does each generation have before the LORD (v 5-6)? God charges each generation with the responsibility to pass on the faith to the generation that follows. We declare to our children (and their generation)—so that they might declare it to their children (and their generation)—who God is and that he has worked a great salvation for his people.

EXPLORE MORE
In groups, read the following sections of Psalm 78 and answer the questions.
- **v 9-31 • v 32-55 • v 56-72**
What is reflected in these verses about the people of God?
What is reflected in these verses about God himself?
Split the larger group into three smaller groups. Assign one of the above portions of Psalm 78 to each small group. Ask them to consider their verses and answer the two questions. Have the group reassemble and share their thoughts with the larger group.
- **v 9-31:** *The people of God* did not keep God's covenant (v 10), forgot his works (v 11), rebelled against him (v 17), tested him (v 18), spoke against him (v 19), did not believe or trust in him (v 22).

God performed wonders in Egypt (v 12), divided the sea for them to pass through (v 13), led them day and night (v 14), gave them water to drink (v 15-16), and bread/manna to eat (v 20, 24), as well as meat (v 27), and killed some of them in his anger (v 31).

- **v 32-55:** *The people of God* did not believe him despite his wonders (v 32), though they sought him, repented and remembered that he was their rock when he killed them (v 34-35), but they insincerely flattered him and lied to him at other times (v 36); they were not steadfast toward him (v 37), they rebelled against him, grieved him, tested and provoked him (v 40-41), and did not remember his power (v 42). *God* atoned for their iniquity, did not destroy them and restrained his anger (v 38), he remembered that they were but flesh (v 39), and he redeemed them from the foe (v 42) by sending plagues against the enemy (v 43-50); he struck down the firstborn in Egypt (v 51), led out his people like sheep and guided them (v 52), kept them safe (v 53), brought them to his holy land (v 54), drove out the nations before them and settled them there (v 55).

- **v 56-72**: *The people of God* tested and rebelled against him and did not keep his commands (v 56), they turned away from him and acted treacherously (v 57), and provoked him to anger by their idolatry (v 58). *God* removed his presence from among them (v 60), and handed them over to be destroyed by their enemies (v 61-64), but he routed the enemies (v 66), and chose David from the tribe of Judah to shepherd his people (v 70-72).

4. Why is Asaph concerned that the next generation teach these lessons (v 7-8)?

The hope is that the next generation, our children, might set their hope in God; that they would come to him in faith, follow his commandments, and not be a rebellious generation. Isn't this the great hope of every Christian parent and passing generation in the church?! We want the next generation not only to "hear", but "know" this God and his salvation (v 3).

5. APPLY: What are the stories that our generation should be telling the generation that comes after us? The same stories from history that we were told: the gospel. It is incumbent upon us that we share the good news of Christ Jesus, this glorious salvation, and the great God who accomplished it. Use this time to discuss with the group the essentials of the Christian faith: God the Creator, man created in God's image, the fall, the promise of a deliverer, the incarnation, the life of Christ, the crucifixion, the resurrection, the ascension, the work of the Spirit, the final judgment, etc.

- **In what ways can we help each other to do this?** This is an opportunity for people in the group to request and to offer help and encouragement in the task of telling the coming generation the glorious deeds of the Lord. This might include: praying together for non-Christian children, young people and others that we or our church has contact with; sharing books and ideas that will help us in telling the gospel; offering support and encouragement to those we know of who have opportunities and responsibilities in this area—youth and children's leaders, Christian students, those involved in community ministries, those with non-Christian family, etc.

6. Paul is reminded of Timothy's faith

(2 Timothy 1 v 5). What characterizes that faith? Paul calls Timothy's faith "sincere." That is, Timothy possesses a genuine faith, unlike the false teachers referred to in 2 Timothy (e.g. 4 v 3). This faith is a gift to Timothy from God—this is stressed by the phrase "dwells in you," which suggests that faith has taken up residence in Timothy. Faith, as we saw in previous studies, is a divine gift, not a human achievement. There is also a sense in which Timothy received this gift of faith from his mother and grandmother. Eunice and Lois held to this same faith and presumably taught Timothy the truth of God and what he has done for his people. This passage provides a wonderful opportunity to highlight the importance Scripture places upon the Christian home and the impact faithful mothers (and grandmothers) can have in the lives of their children. (Obviously, fathers can as well—note Deuteronomy 6).

7. Why should every Christian mother, grandmother, father, husband, neighbor, and co-worker want to share the faith with those around them? We possess the greatest gift in the universe: Christ himself. We know his beauty, his truth, his peace, his love, his joy, his life… If we truly love others, we will want to share his truth with them that they might know him and enjoy him forever.

8. Of what is Paul "not ashamed," do you think (v 12)? Most likely, Paul is reflecting upon his imprisonment and suffering for the sake of the gospel and boldly declaring that even in such circumstances he knows no shame. See also verse 8. You may want to take this opportunity to probe with the group why we often hold back from sharing the gospel. What are the major obstacles? More often

than not, some sense of shame or fear inhibits us.

- **Why is Paul not ashamed (v 12)?** He knows in whom he has believed. He believes in the Lord and King of glory, who proves to be trustworthy. There will be a day when Paul receives the crown of glory, so the present sufferings of this world are worth enduring. And on that judgment day, it will be those who forsook Christ who will be ashamed, and those who willingly suffered for his glory in this life who will be exalted.

⌄

- **In what ways does your culture pressure you to feel ashamed about the gospel?** Get people to share from their experience what most pressures them to feel ashamed of the gospel.

9. What great assurance does Paul provide at the end of verse 12? Paul assures Timothy that God will guard the faith until the last day. Yes, persecution will strike the church, false teachers will rise in its midst, and the world will mock the Christian faith, but the faith will persevere until that last day. "The gates of hell" shall not prevail against it (Matthew 16 v 18).

10. How does this assurance not lessen the responsibility that Christians bear to preserve and pass on this faith to others (v 13-14)? God preserves the faith, but he chooses to do so through us—Paul tells Timothy to "guard" what has been entrusted to him. We have been given a sacred trust by God and by the previous generation who passed the faith on to us. Now we are entrusted with the responsibility of keeping this faith pure and passing it on to the generation that follows. And this ministry, like all Christian ministry, is accomplished with the help of the Holy Spirit at work within and through us (v 14).

EXPLORE MORE
Read the following passages from Paul's pastoral letters and discuss his concerns in them:

- **1 Timothy 6 v 3-5:** Paul outlines the character of those who refuse to agree with Christ's teaching.

- **1 Timothy 6 v 20-21:** Paul underlines the need to avoid "irreverent babble" and false "knowledge."

- **2 Timothy 3 v 14-17:** Paul sets out the importance of continuing in the teaching of the Scriptures, and why we can have confidence in God's word

- **2 Timothy 4 v 1-5:** Paul charges Timothy to be faithful in preaching the word to people in a time when they don't want to hear it.

- **Titus 2 v 1:** Paul instructs Titus to "teach what accords with sound doctrine."

- **Titus 3 v 9-11:** Paul encourages Titus to insist on Christians believing and living out the truths of the gospel, and warns him to avoid dissension and divisive people.

11. APPLY: Why is it essential that we communicate the doctrinal truths contained in the five *Solas* of the Reformation to the generation that follows us? What is lost if we don't?
The five *Solas* are not mere inconsequential doctrines; they articulate the very heart of the gospel. If we abandon these truths, we abandon the gospel. If we ignore the five *Solas*, we ignore the gospel. If we forget these teachings, we forget the gospel. They must be preserved and passed on, if we are going to be faithful in our generation.

12. APPLY: How did you first hear the truths of the gospel?
- **How does your story, and the stories of others in your group, motivate you all to be actively aiming to pass on the gospel yourselves?**
This serves as a wonderful closing exercise for the group study. Take a little time to briefly hear each person's story. As these testimonies are given, remind the group of God's faithfulness and the faithfulness of those who dared to preserve and pass on the faith they received.

Good Book Guides
The full range

Romans 8–16: 7 Studies
Timothy Keller
ISBN: 9781910307311

1 Corinthians 1–9:
7 Studies
Mark Dever
ISBN: 9781908317681

1 Corinthians 10–16:
8 Studies
Mark Dever & Carl Laferton
ISBN: 9781908317964

1 Corinthians:
8 Studies
Andrew Wilson
ISBN: 9781784986254

2 Corinthians:
7 Studies
Gary Millar
ISBN: 9781784983895

Galatians: 7 Studies
Timothy Keller
ISBN: 9781908762566

Ephesians: 10 Studies
Thabiti Anyabwile
ISBN: 9781907377099

Ephesians: 8 Studies
Richard Coekin
ISBN: 9781910307694

Philippians: 7 Studies
Steven J. Lawson
ISBN: 9781784981181

Colossians: 6 Studies
Mark Meynell
ISBN: 9781906334246

1 Thessalonians:
7 Studies
Mark Wallace
ISBN: 9781904889533

1&2 Timothy: 7 Studies
Phillip Jensen
ISBN: 9781784980191

Titus: 5 Studies
Tim Chester
ISBN: 9781909919631

Hebrews: 8 Studies
Michael J. Kruger
ISBN: 9781784986049

James: 6 Studies
Sam Allberry
ISBN: 9781910307816

1 Peter: 6 Studies
Juan R. Sanchez
ISBN: 9781784980177

2 Peter & Jude: 6 Studies
Miguel Núñez
ISBN: 9781784987121

1 John: 7 Studies
Nathan Buttery
ISBN: 9781904889953

Revelation: 7 Studies
Tim Chester
ISBN: 9781910307021

TOPICAL

Man of God: 10 Studies
Anthony Bewes & Sam Allberry
ISBN: 9781904889977

Biblical Womanhood:
10 Studies
Sarah Collins
ISBN: 9781907377532

The Apostles' Creed:
10 Studies
Tim Chester
ISBN: 9781905564415

Promises Kept: Bible Overview: 9 Studies
Carl Laferton
ISBN: 9781908317933

The Reformation Solas
6 Studies
Jason Helopoulos
ISBN: 9781784981501

Contentment: 6 Studies
Anne Woodcock
ISBN: 9781905564668

Women of Faith:
8 Studies
Mary Davis
ISBN: 9781904889526

Meeting Jesus: 8 Studies
Jenna Kavonic
ISBN: 9781905564460

Heaven: 6 Studies
Andy Telfer
ISBN: 9781909919457

Making Work Work:
8 Studies
Marcus Nodder
ISBN: 9781908762894

The Holy Spirit: 8 Studies
Pete & Anne Woodcock
ISBN: 9781905564217

Experiencing God:
6 Studies
Tim Chester
ISBN: 9781906334437

Real Prayer: 7 Studies
Anne Woodcock
ISBN: 9781910307595

Mission: 7 Studies
Alan Purser
ISBN: 9781784983628

Church: 8 Studies
Anne Woodcock
ISBN: 9781784984199

Talking to Our Father:
7 Studies
Tim Chester
ISBN: 9781784985202

The Whole Series

- **Exodus For You** *Tim Chester*
- **Judges For You** *Timothy Keller*
- **Ruth For You** *Tony Merida*
- **1 Samuel For You** *Tim Chester*
- **2 Samuel For You** *Tim Chester*
- **Nehemiah For You** *Eric Mason*
- **Psalms For You** *Christopher Ash*
- **Proverbs For You** *Kathleen Nielson*
- **Isaiah For You** *Tim Chester*
- **Daniel For You** *David Helm*
- **Micah For You** *Stephen Um*
- **Mark For You** *Jason Meyer*
- **Luke 1-12 For You** *Mike McKinley*
- **Luke 12-24 For You** *Mike McKinley*
- **John 1-12 For You** *Josh Moody*
- **John 13-21 For You** *Josh Moody*
- **Acts 1-12 For You** *Albert Mohler*
- **Acts 13-28 For You** *Albert Mohler*

- **Romans 1-7 For You** *Timothy Keller*
- **Romans 8-16 For You** *Timothy Keller*
- **1 Corinthians For You** *Andrew Wilson*
- **2 Corinthians For You** *Gary Millar*
- **Galatians For You** *Timothy Keller*
- **Ephesians For You** *Richard Coekin*
- **Philippians For You** *Steven Lawson*
- **Colossians & Philemon For You** *Mark Meynell*
- **1 & 2 Timothy For You** *Phillip Jensen*
- **Titus For You** *Tim Chester*
- **Hebrews For You** *Michael Kruger*
- **James For You** *Sam Allberry*
- **1 Peter For You** *Juan Sanchez*
- **2 Peter & Jude For You** *Miguel Núñez*
- **Revelation For You** *Tim Chester*

Find out more about these resources at:

www.thegoodbook.com/for-you
www.thegoodbook.co.uk/for-you

thegoodbook
COMPANY

BIBLICAL | RELEVANT | ACCESSIBLE

At The Good Book Company, we are dedicated to helping Christians and local churches grow. We believe that God's growth process always starts with hearing clearly what he has said to us through his timeless word—the Bible.

Ever since we opened our doors in 1991, we have been striving to produce Bible-based resources that bring glory to God. We have grown to become an international provider of user-friendly resources to the Christian community, with believers of all backgrounds and denominations using our books, Bible studies, devotionals, evangelistic resources, and DVD-based courses.

We want to equip ordinary Christians to live for Christ day by day, and churches to grow in their knowledge of God, their love for one another, and the effectiveness of their outreach.

Call us for a discussion of your needs or visit one of our local websites for more information on the resources and services we provide.

Your friends at The Good Book Company

thegoodbook.com | thegoodbook.co.uk
thegoodbook.com.au | thegoodbook.co.nz
thegoodbook.co.in